CHINA LOOKS
at the WORLD

François Geoffroy-Dechaume

CHINA LOOKS at the WORLD

Reflections for a dialogue:
eight letters to T'ang-lin

Translated from the French by Jean Stewart

With an Introduction by Paul Mus
PROFESSOR OF FAR EASTERN CIVILIZATIONS
AT THE COLLÈGE DE FRANCE AND YALE UNIVERSITY

and a Foreword by

The Right Honourable Philip Noel-Baker

PANTHEON BOOKS
A Division of Random House
NEW YORK

Contents

CONTENTS

Illustrations

' "But China obscures," you say; and
I reply, "China obscures, but there
is light to be found. Look for it." '

PASCAL, Pensées, 397 (159)

On the Cultural Revolution

Culture is the main theme of this book. The "cultural revolution" in China in 1966 has shown some of the power of this word, though not its full meaning.

Culture, it has been said, is what remains when all is forgotten. To Westerners it conveys, in its basic sense, the peaceful act of ploughing; to China, it means much more.

A century ago an American captain, although his country was not at war, gave support to the British in a sea battle off the China coast. He later justified himself by saying that "blood is thicker than water."

Whatever the meaning of Culture, one should today ponder, and act, on the assumption that Culture is thicker than blood.

F.G-D.

FOREWORD

by

the Rt. Hon. Philip Noel-Baker, M.P.,

awarded Nobel Peace Prize, 1959

FRANÇOIS GEOFFROY-DECHAUME is a painter, as well as a government official and an author. He has written a book which is learned, penetrating and wise; but which, above all, is instinct with the life and thinking of the Chinese people about whom he writes, and among whom he lived and worked for thirty years.

It is an artist's book, in the elegance of his synthesis, and of his use of words. But the profound importance of his basic theme makes it a book for everyone who cares about the future peace and happiness of mankind.

M. Geoffroy-Dechaume's purpose is to make 'Westerners' understand the vast significance of China in the society of states; the true meaning of the Chinese Revolution of 1949; and the grave dangers that may result from Western misconceptions about China, and Chinese misconceptions about the West. He wants us to see ourselves as China sees us; he wants China to see the good which the West can offer, not only the violence and corruption they have suffered at Western hands in the past.

Few people in the West have really grasped the fact that China has had a great civilization for three thousand years, and that for more than two thousand she was a model of good government, founded on the precepts and philosophy of the great Confucius. Confucius, who lived five hundred years before Jesus Christ, first said: 'What you do not want done to yourself do not to others'. He taught that every man should develop not only his own deeply-rooted individuality, but also a deep sense of responsibility towards others, a sense of the unity of all men. Confucius believed that any use of force was a confession of failure; that violence, against man or nature, was wrong; and war a form of violence evil in the ultimate degree.

II

In China's history there have been revolutions and invasions, bad emperors and wicked ministers. But Confucianism has always triumphed; the conquerors were absorbed into the Chinese civilization; after each revolution, each change of dynasty, Confucian ethics and Confucian teaching remained the foundation of the new régime. Confucianism has been a principle of Commonwealth which has knit the various Chinese nations together in what M. Geoffroy-Dechaume calls a 'civilization-state'—a 'civilization-state' which is showing today, after two-and-a-half millennia, its immense vitality and unifying power. Even since the Marxist revolution of 1949, Confucianism remains a wholly extraordinary moral force; it still largely forms the thinking and the character of everyone who calls himself Chinese.

M. Geoffroy-Dechaume writes with sympathetic insight about many other aspects of the Chinese genius. He studies the impact on this genius of the Western Marxism which the leaders of the Long March put into practice in 1949. And he says: 'To grasp the nature and significance of the Chinese Revolution is as important for world peace as all our efforts for "development" or disarmament.'

Important for world peace? M. Geoffroy-Dechaume is obsessed, as we all should be, by the danger of a sinister new fact. In all its long history since Confucius compiled his Five Books, no Emperor of China, no Chinese statesman, has ever spoken a single word in praise of war. But now Mao Tse-tung has done so. What may this portend for the future of mankind? By what bitter grievance against the capitalism of the West are his words inspired?

A personal memory helps me to understand the nature of the sustained and passionate 'revulsion' against the West which M. Geoffroy-Dechaume describes. I was taught at school by a History master that the blackest crimes of Imperial Britain were the 'Opium Wars' of 1839 to 1862; the wars in which Britain, with troops and warships, defeated the resolute attempts of Chinese Emperors to stamp out the vice of opium smoking, and at length compelled them to legalize the sale and use of the

pernicious drug throughout their Imperial domain. At the end
of the First World War, I came straight back from the Front
to the Peace Conference in Paris. There I met an eminent member of the British delegation, Sir John Jordan, who had lived for
forty years in China, and had risen to be Minister (i.e. Ambassa-
dor) in Peking. When I asked him why China had then fallen
into civil war and chaos, and why its famous and ancient system
of government had broken down, his reply was brief and
devastating: 'Opium smoking.'

Chinese officials, of all ranks, Sir John explained, had fallen
victim to this insidious vice; their vigour, their efficiency and
their integrity had been fatally undermined. While China was
thus weakened, the West took every chance to exploit and to
humiliate her. 'Unequal treaties'; the rape of whole provinces;
'zones of influence'; 'concessions' in which the government of
whole cities was given to foreigners; 'extra-territoriality'—
special courts for foreigners outside the Chinese law; railways
and other national enterprises built by foreign capital, and man-
aged, for foreign profit, by foreign control; Japanese aggressions, inspired by the doctrines of Western militarist imperialism,
and carried out with Western arms—all this left the Chinese
people feeling crushed and desperate and helpless.

Their first attempts at change and reform led only to disunity
and strife. For four decades of civil war, till the Long March
triumphed in 1949, the War Lords looted and massacred the
people, always with unlimited supplies of Western arms. After
their conquest of Manchuria in 1932, unresisted by the League
of Nations, the Japanese militarists started giving heroin injec-
tions to Chinese boys and girls at school, and by similar infamies
sought to execute their plan of Asian Co-prosperity, that is, the
conquest of the whole of China.

It was from this long record of Western wrongs that Mao
Tse-tung carried through his 'liberation' of the Chinese people.
He, and they, could only see that Western capitalists had brought
them indignities, violence and corruption in almost every form.

This explains the tragic end of M. Geoffroy-Dechaume's
letters to T'ang-lin. Long ago, they were as close as brothers.

But as the Revolution began to gain the mastery of T'ang-lin's mind, so, little by little, he walked on the other side of the street; so he wanted to reject *everything* the West could give.

But this may spell disaster for the human race. Six hundred and fifty million Chinese, as many as the United States, Western Europe and the Soviet Union combined; greatly gifted, masters already of the science and technology of the West, with vast natural resources—what may this mean in twenty years from now, if, with a new and ardent faith, China should be militarized as Japan was militarized before the Second World War?

M. Geoffroy-Dechaume's appeal is unanswerable. There is no time to lose. We must *prove* to China that the West does not stand for power-politics and private profit. We must start to unwind the long coil of misunderstanding produced by the Western errors of the last century and a half. We must seek to understand the greatness of China, as she must learn to understand the true glories of the West. Together we must conquer all the formidable obstacles which separate us, and must create a new world-wide system of mutual tolerance, world-wide disarmament, and permanent peace. If M. Geoffroy-Dechaume helps us to succeed in this endeavour, he will have served his generation well.

INTRODUCTION

Towards a Chinese view of Descartes

by

Paul Mus

Professor of Oriental Studies

at the Collège de France and Yale University

T'ANG-LIN is knocking at the door. Who is T'ang-lin? A Chinese, who really exists, as we are told by his friend M. Geoffroy-Dechaume, and to whom eight letters in this book are addressed. Yes, but there are 650 million others like him, and there lies the problem. Their voice is too loud to allow us to relapse readily into our dogmatic slumber. Yet how much longer will it take us to learn to see ourselves with 'the eyes of the Other'? Sartre's phrase designates that detached look whose virtue he has demonstrated, in anticipation of a still unachieved total humanism that look which China now turns on us, not troubling over-much about what our own view of ourselves and of her may be. As our author plainly reminds us, this Chinese vision of Europe, through the chain-reactions involved in the confrontation, is as much part of what Europe is as Europe's vision of herself. The whole will be needed to make up one world.

We must not lay too much stress here on the word *Europe*. China thinks rather of the West. This, too, is T'ang-lin's message through his impartial and perceptive correspondent. The West includes America and the U.S.S.R.—China needs the whole of that, and needs it fundamentally, before she can feel herself confronted with a partner of her own stature.

And yet, despite this widening of her approach, China's quarrel remains, in a sense, chiefly with Europe proper. Asiatic thought, indeed, is neither discursive, nor even, on principle, logical, but primarily genealogical. It follows in this the logic of existence, instead of the logic of ideas. This is why China tends

15

to conceive all Western peoples in terms of their common origin, while she seeks to confront them as a whole. For she sees in herself, at this turning-point of history, the potential source of the rest of the world—of another world, rather, of which 'the West' would merely be the remainder. Bloc versus bloc, with Asia the core of mankind—plus Africa, if the course of events strengthens, as it promises to do, the moral ties between these two continents; this other community would be more than even with us!

Such is China's programme, in which the room and role allotted to the 'Europe that the Chinese see' are liable, consequently, to resemble the share that only yesterday Europe allotted to the Chinese. It is now for them to try and form a juster judgement than ours.

It is not amid the excitement of present action but by a reassessment of either side's sources that an attempt at mutual understanding might be made, on the lines suggested in M. Geoffroy-Dechaume's book. He provides moreover a sample of what he proposes, since his book is based on long years of familiarity with China, and since it manifestly speaks with the accents of a successful friendship between men.

In an endeavour to get thus closer to the 'historical' essence of our being, when I read M. Geoffroy-Dechaume's quotation from Pascal I could imagine a test which would go further than might be supposed at first sight; expressed in simple terms: *let T'ang-lin*—or his son—*give us a Chinese view of Descartes*. This would be the necessary complement enabling this essential author to guide us to what is most 'logical' in ourselves, to attain the stature which is his by right, and which eventually will be acknowledged by humanists all over the world; thanks to such a Chinese contribution, Descartes' thought would shed new light on himself and on ourselves, as well as on Asia.

For the time being, Descartes' readers and commentators can be assessed according to the angle from which they prove capable of approaching him. It must be admitted that if he sought to model the French University—the Sorbonne—on his own image, it has returned the compliment. The Descartes whom we praise and teach reflects more of our own features than of his. Eastern thinkers—I mean those who are fully Eastern, essentially the Chinese and the Indians, and not a Western fringe in Asia Minor—would thus be justified in taking him as an example of what they find most reprehensible in us, namely of having divorced *man* from what man conceives and also, as an inevitable consequence, from what man constructs.

For Descartes withdraws from everything and rebuilds a world, but a world without weight (in a literal sense since Newton had not yet appeared) starting from things which are, in his view, the simplest—thus, first of all, himself ('myself, that's to say my soul') and going on to the most composite, even assuming an order to exist among those which do not proceed naturally from one another. The text has become a classic one. Eastern thinkers are justifiably amazed that after this insolent attitude of Descartes' towards authentic logic we should still offer him as an example of it. But be careful! If our opinions conflict on this subject, perhaps we are 'obscuring' China in the matter as much as she 'obscures' us. Does she not indeed tend to see this master of thought through our discipleship, instead of forming her own view of him, and thus enriching all of us?

China may rightly reproach us for having reached the point, with Descartes as *we* see him, of mistaking enumerations for real things, and in particular, voting papers for peoples (whether or not China's criticism is finally justified on this last issue need not be discussed here); adding furthermore that whatever treats of things as a whole without application to anything in particular—*nulli speciali materiae*, the *Regulae* decree—solves nothing, and that moreover whatever is addressed, or supposes itself addressed, to all mankind indiscriminately appeals only to those who are already convinced; and of this the two-thirds of humanity which China believes are behind her in that respect would here provide the counter-proof! A telling phrase of M. Geoffroy-Dechaume's may perhaps be applied to the author of the *Discours de la Méthode*, when China comes to see him better on her own account, as well as to European thought in general: that 'our failure to understand the Chinese starts with a failure to understand ourselves.' They must have a share in us, as we are to have in them—when T'ang-lin answers!

One implication of Descartes' logic, according to this view, would lie at the root of the conflict of civilizations which forms the background of the present work, viz. what the modern world has learnt to call *the position of the privileged observer*. Descartes would have made this method out of the very thing that our more advanced sciences today invite us to consider as an unpardonable sin against method.

But is this really Descartes? Will this be the Chinese view of him? If I may be allowed, for the sake of argument, to forecast what that view might be—remembering for instance early childish contacts my first friends, Lin Y-meo and Lin Y-mu who, with Hu-ko, used to introduce themselves formally as 'the three sons, one of them a nephew' of a high mandarin in the service of the then Emperor, this other Descartes would prove more 'genealogical' in true Chinese fashion, and thus more consistent with himself than the West usually makes him (as a careful reading will reveal).

To justify basically what seems 'simple' to him, Descartes takes his stand, in fact, on the culture and the society 'in which God has granted him to be born'. It takes a deep belief in a Creator God, as Absolute Unity, and in created 'souls' conceived to have been made in His image, to assert that 'I (i.e. my soul) am the simplest thing, from which I ought to start'. But as soon as this condition is explicitly accepted as such, with its implied limitations, then, contrary to what people have so often tried to read into Descartes, this frank and open admission renders his criterion of clarity and distinction unimpeachable at his own level, so long as one takes into account the historic circumstances to which he refers us, that is to say the semantic system, the grammar, as it were, of a culture within whose framework he deliberately confines both himself and, consequently, his readers, for instance when he quotes as his final authority St. Anselm and the Rule of Eminence.

The mistake of his followers has been usually to see in this reference only lip service cautiously paid to the established Church, whereas the Father of modern Philosophy saw in it a pattern of universal thinking, inherited from ancient Asian civilizations through Graeco-Roman traditions. Its secular, juridical counterpart is still attainable if not familiar, under the name and concept of *Eminent Domain*: 'Lordship of sovereign power over all property in the State, with right of expropriation', to quote a popular lexical entry. This is precisely the spirit in which Descartes in the last resort surrendered his reason, not to restrict it, but on the contrary to provide it with a fully universal guarantee, independent of and elevated above local circumstances. As distinct from the relative, applied universality of reason, i.e. reason faithful to itself in an endeavour to match given circumstances, its absolute universality, implying, covering and commanding all possible instances is beyond our reach; moreover we do not need, in our own limited circumstances, what belongs to other instances: this is God's privilege, vividly called Eminence. Applied, relative universality, however, still has in it what entitles us to maintain that appellation, as all 'reasonable' creatures, although they may act quite differently in other settings, would act as we do, were they conditioned as we are by our special background—religious, cultural, semantic, sociological and so on. One might call this the universal *distributivity* of reason, rather than its direct universal *validity*. By his profession of faith, Descartes submits to that imposing cosmic pattern and clearly and distinctly assumes it, irrespective of particular circumstances.

Anticipating by three centuries our own age and its œcumenical dilemmas, this Descartes, new for us but henceforward belonging to the whole world's culture, implicitly warns us that if such ultimate criteria were to come into conflict (as Pascal also had foreseen, 'But China obscures . . .') the first step for each of us would be to reassess ourselves in our own role as men, starting in each case from the very beginning, remaining consistent with our own particular background and always acting according to the best wisdom it provides, due account being taken of our limitations. This is clearly suggested by a comparison between Descartes' reliance on God's Eminence and his bold and fine image of the way out of the forest, a wager on humanity as against the direct wager on God to which Pascal had confined himself. Let us bet on God's existence, Pascal advises us. If we lose, there was nothing to lose. If we win, we win all. But once Descartes, lost in an unknown and uncharted forest, has determined to the best of his capacity the direction in which to try to escape, he gives as the crucial rule: if no new information turns up in the process, never deviate from the line first taken. Now what kind of a reasoning is this? If the initial decision is wrong, Descartes forsakes all chance of correcting it. Such being the case, he loses all. Yes, but if such a rule is steadily applied in all circumstances, *statistically*, the partakers of this kind of covenant of reason with itself will benefit by it.

Quite a 'Confucian' approach, indeed! Can anything be further from a pretension to what modern science critically calls the position of the privileged observer?

Ask yourself the question, as you read the scrupulously critical and open-minded pages that follow. Imagine, then, T'ang-lin's reply, inspired by human friendship. For have no doubt, it will come, and it will be decisive, whatever form history may impose on it. You will compare it, when the time comes, with M. Geoffroy-Dechaume's provisional presentation, all the more stimulating for being anticipatory. You will probably discover that we have only gone half-way, but that the Chinese counterpart, on the other hand, could have done no more. Now that is exactly what we need to raise 'eminence', i.e. our ultimate criterion, to where it ought to be, whether we call it God, Tao or Dharma, and then to adjust our ways to one another without further delay. Don't we need this complete base in order to build the apex?

This sounds like high philosophy, no doubt, and M. Geoffroy-Dechaume does not seek to deny the fact, although the word sometimes arouses apprehensions. But his is a human philosophy which, far from leading us away from the concrete, brings us back to it by all manner of mutually enriching paths. After all, cannot the so-called 'technique of enrichment', which is so eminently a question of the day, enable us, if we choose our material well, to build a better world, instead of exclusively preparing a more complete destruction? This sums up the whole of our age, uneasily poised between two gigantic *plus* and *minus* signs, both world-wide!

Take this book with you then, whether you go to China yourself as it will encourage you to do, or whether you choose the easier way opened up by other contributions to our knowledge of present-day China, also based on living experience but from a different angle, giving precedence to facts over evaluations. You will find however quite a few which are rich in implicit philosophy under a wealth of concrete notations—for instance the pencilled sketches brought back from his latest journey by Robert Guillain. Trying my hand at Asiatic logic, I would venture to say that his book and this one together make up far more than the sum of what each says separately.

Can the two kinds of insight be fitted together? Perhaps it is better to train and discipline oneself to come and go freely between the two styles, as though passing from one world to another. Such, indeed, are the two ways of approaching the world as re-centred on China, a world which consists for the present more of movements than of achievements, more of problems than of conclusions. We must then not attempt a hasty synthesis, but learn to balance the evidence provided by the complete objectivity of a broad, detached and intelligent reportage such as Guillain's against an inward vision like that of T'ang-lin's friend, which strives furthermore towards a twofold inwardness, by sustained self-criticism and by that 'view through the eyes of the Other' which makes that kind of confrontation possible, and indeed inevitable.

For there is conversely much living concrete experience of China to be found in M. Geoffroy-Dechaume's book too, as he takes us through the streets and parks of Peking, shows us its gates and its temples at different seasons; or again in his penetrating and picturesque evocation of the Chinese seascape, with its population of fishers and sailors and its fleet of tall junks, somewhat akin to the well-known *Propos* in which Alain describes the Breton tunny-fishers as a condensed reflection of the wind, the power of the waves, and man's slow effort, disciplined by these, to conquer them: *non nisi parendo*. . . .

'Those high sterns recalling our historic galleons, the outline of the hulls, the tilt of the masts, the arrangement of the sails, all told of a highly perfected art of navigation and explained its contagious success. I have seen such vessels, which are said to have reached Arabia as early as the thirteenth century, throughout the Chinese world and even in mid-Pacific. Their shape has a changeless quality, as if they were a biological species which only some mutation could transform. These boats, typically Chinese shapes—among so many others—are, like your porcelain ware, a technical expression of living China. Your famous workmanship is not a thing of the past . . .'

'. . . the economy and efficiency of the Chinese workman's action and the excellence of its result astonish one. To reach such a point more was needed, surely, than the mere accumulation of time, more even than a tradition of work whose effectiveness has been confirmed through long centuries. The shape of boats or roofs corresponds to mental attitudes and to a conception of the world. It represents the worker's dialogue with wood and water, but it also reflects the long, slow intermingling of instinctive, popular wisdom with learned thought . . . .

'. . . Thus around any tangible invention there cluster invisible inventions. We are wholly steeped in our techniques. Just as China has her junks and her tea, she has her own forms of economy, of politics, of thought and of hope. Anything she borrows she immediately adapts, so that the whole may retain, or recover, its original aspect. . . .

'. . . But today a violent storm is raging, as you know, because certain techniques, not only mechanical ones, are spreading over the globe, bringing an invisible train in their wake. . . .

'You, in China, thought you could separate scientific technique from its train. As soon as she had borrowed guns, China became caught up in the whole network of arsenals, schools and democratic methods, believing at each stage that she could still preserve her essential values. You have touched the bottom of the abyss. You have felt the cold breath of nothingness. Hence your revulsive crisis.

'The whole fleet of your invisible junks stands face to face with the fleet of our vessels in a titanic struggle. I see those great ships, your wisdom and your ethics, half unmasted, springing a leak, while their crews try to reach land on makeshift boats. You organize your defences, you block all approaches, you grasp science and try to conciliate it, seeing in it a liberating force for yourselves against cultural and moral servitude and a means of revenge, but also a necessary instrument for the construction of your modern world.'

This is the essential part of what T'ang-lin will teach us to see, for it is a fact that grows clearer every day that neither we nor Soviet Marxism, from which China has derived so much, can deprive her of that vital and invisible wealth which not only belongs to her but makes her. Our author quotes with reference to the 'economic' rather than national background of the Chinese peasantry, a saying of Mao Tse-tung's which had already struck me as throwing vivid light on the parallel experience of Vietnam. 'The strength of the peasant class is like that of raging winds or torrential rain. Its violence increases rapidly, and no power on earth can check it; the peasant class will tear down any chains that bind it, it will rush forward on the road to freedom. It will trample underfoot all Imperialist forces, militarism, corrupt officials, village bigwigs and landlords. All revolutionary parties, all fellow-travellers will be subject to examination by it, and it will either accept them or reject them. Shall we be in the vanguard to lead this peasant class, or shall we lag behind, in opposition to it?'

The ultimate truth is to be found in the living masses, trained to be true to themselves and not to abstract ideas. 'Don't take away the value of one man'—this phrase, noted once by Alain in a dispute between proletarians, sums up our misunderstanding of Asia. We can understand thus how the 'third world' accuses us today of cultural aggression when we naïvely proclaim our intention—taking the capacity for granted—of feeding it. The settlement can no longer be postponed. Not *Dans Trente Ans la Chine*, but *From now onwards, the Chinese* . . . neither the 'Chinamen' we despised yesterday, nor tomorrow's dreaded robots, as M. Geoffroy-Dechaume cogently reminds us! That is the way towards man's reintegration, both in our own countries and in China, even while the road seems dark.

On this ever-shrinking planet, there is no choice but to take it as a whole. Whatever our doctrinal differences, however essential we may think our own views, nevertheless, when one takes due account of the existential background which is common to all of us within that setting, to leave out China, a China re-evaluated on the firm base of her essential nature of which in *China Looks at the World* we catch a glimpse, would be to lose a part of ourselves that reaches far deeper than our ideologies. We seem to have neglected it, but we are beginning to rediscover it today when we look at ourselves through 'the eyes of the Other',—for every move brings us back to that Sartrian rule of rules. As is said here, with as much courage as perception, the things we fail to understand about China are those that we have already lost within ourselves. It is certain then that what we shall learn from this new contact will not be merely a Marxism more intransigent than that of the Russians, as so many Westerners fear. In fact, to quote M. Geoffroy-Dechaume's illuminating comment, 'Communism conceals China from us'. Is it not highly significant that a remarkable American expert, Dr. Robert Blum, should have quite independently reached the same conclusion? There will be much to be learnt from the long-awaited posthumous publication of his analysis, made for the influential Council on Foreign Relations, which can scarcely be suspected of a bias in favour of 'Mainland' China! To see clearly into ourselves as well as into China it is most desirable, at this precise point in the controversy, that *China Looks at the World* should encourage us, men of the West, to look back over the landmarks of our own past and to realign ourselves—and the Chinese with us—according to our new views. Should we derive therefrom no other benefit than a better understanding of what has made us what we are, so that we may find ourselves sometimes close to cultures from which we believed ourselves most remote, it would be valuable on that account alone to add a 'Chinese' Descartes to the usual academic version. Seen against the exact background of his period, of which his followers have usually taken too little account, he assumes a more normal humanity, giving explicit moral significance even to his geometry: by no means an abstraction or an incomplete personality, but a whole man, contributing to his own time through science indeed, but first of all for the sake of action. This is what a Chinese view would give us as a first lesson, by analogy with China's own background. For if Descartes is a natural product of France, this image should inevitably evoke the soil of France, made up, as is the soil of China, of all the actions of those who have tilled it: behind the *Méditations*, as we are reminded by that eminent geographer Roupnel, lies the 'invisible cortège' of our history.

The contribution made by M. Geoffroy-Dechaume to this difficult, painful and necessary debate now becomes clear: it is that of a moralist, in realms where our two nations, in so far as one can call China just a nation, have always had some affinity. The plan, here, breaks deliberately with conventional forms: the unity we discover in it, as we grow familiar with it, is in fact *man*, that closest unity of all, somewhat as in the case of the *Maximes* and the *Pensées*, the author's great models. We must admire—and the Chinese, skilled artists in this genre, will surely appreciate—phrases such as these:

'There is no better or finer fiction than the reality of others.'

'In your poor but patient villages, where we were so often welcomed with the courtesy that you, T'ang-lin, know so well, with that sort of absolute dignity conferred by unremitting labour borne loftily, I learned to distinguish between poverty and destitution.'

'The individual sums up everything, but only within his milieu . . .'

Such well-coined epigrams readily provide highly profitable cultural view-points, commanding ample perspectives and invaluable cross-references: a welcome halt, until one resumes the trek.

In these pages, the first thing that strikes one is that each point is dealt with thrice over. In each case there is:

— a prelude, which sets forth in a general fashion certain facts about China in relation to the whole of the Far East, from South-East Asia to Japan;

— an analysis, detailed and predominantly comparative, of the Western and Chinese data; this is the main part of the book;

— a letter, which resumes the dominant themes in less detail but not less forcibly, most often in the form of an interlude depicting the scene of some past experience, and so powerfully that one finds oneself listening for the answers to the questions which the Western writer puts so urgently to his Chinese friend.

Can one object to these repetitions? One might as well object to the imitations in a piece of counterpoint—and moreover the gain in critical clarity is enough to justify the method. As M. Geoffroy-Dechaume advises us, to read the letters first and then come back to the analysis is an easy and rewarding way of tackling his theme.

His book is further divided into eight sections, which again are not bound by our usual categories, so that it may be helpful to stress their sequence here.

1. *Revolution.* This commonplace word is used chiefly in order to be replaced by the much more specific term *revulsive crisis*, which implies the total reaction of every Chinese, throughout China, to the long humiliation endured by her through contacts which to our discomfiture we hear described as 'cultural aggression'.

2. *China in perspective.* Pertinent comments on the role of Chinese writing in this conflict between two semantic systems.

3. *China envisaged.* What the eye sees, on either side; these

outward and visible signs are here in fact deliberately taken as a basis for passing judgment on the observer as well as on the thing observed.

4. *Technique.* The word is used in the singular with didactic intention: besides the manifold techniques applied to matter, but at this stage of craftsmanship making use chiefly of man's hand and brain, he considers the special technique of conditioning man to their use.

5. *The Individual.* Only after completing this study of man from the outside, where he is just as clearly present as in his innermost being, does one fully grasp what his personality is under the circumstances.

6. *Music.* Under this heading the arts are reviewed, and the suggestion made that the theatre is the essential art for China, since it envisages man not in relation to a Creator but as established in the centre of a creation whose harmonies he feels and expresses: all the world's a stage for him.

7. *Thought.* Here more than ever a concern with concreteness is evident. After dealing under the six previous headings with all that affects us through our senses, we come to thought; yet special stress is laid not on abstractions but on the 'existential shock' felt by the best Western minds on contact with Chinese civilization.

8. *Passions.* Here we come to the end of this *gradus ad Parnassum.* Let us not however proclaim too hastily that the Chinese set the irrational above reason. The truth is that they recognize reason in that cosmic happening which is the people, image of the world: this consummation is set 'en bloc' against the dualism of mind and matter that commands our own perspectives. From this pre-established total, everything logically proceeds contrary to the Cartesian sequence—when considered apart from the way Descartes carefully refers it to God's 'Eminence', another expression of the pre-established cosmic total, with which it would not be so difficult to reconcile the usual Confucian imagery. In a word, it finally means conceiving man as a self-governing whole within a whole, in the cosmos, that is not '*in abstracto*' but at the point and moment when he 'happens'.

Although M. Geoffroy-Dechaume is discreet in his philosophical references, we can perceive one here whose scope is too important amid the cultural changes which may be preparing tomorrow's world-humanism, not to be given all the stress it will bear. *China Looks at the World*, in fact, makes us start from an event, or, to use a more modern term, a happening: China's humiliation, as we have said, which increased over the centuries through contact with Western 'arrogance'; hence her revulsive crisis! Here, in fact, is where with M. Geoffroy-Dechaume's items 7 (Thought) and 8 (Passions) we reach the term of the progression. After having been through all the human elements involved, starting from the Chinese collective 'revulsion', the 'happening' finally takes the form of an inner experience. But, and this is the point not to be missed, this inner experience of the individual fits into what 'happens' to the whole group, a group which in this case is not a nation but a 'Civilization-State'. For we have to reconcile ourselves to the idea that such is China, with its tendency to include everything in this world as a counterpart to and liquidation of what our own claim may once have been. This Chinese solidarity with the whole world, inscribed by her within the individual as his essential formula, reminds us once again—but perhaps with a deeper understanding—that they will be neither 'Chinamen' nor 'robots', but men!

'Four characters are today inscribed on classroom walls, above the blackboard in schools where more than a hundred million pupils absorb their message. "Listen to the word of the Party!" This slogan would not have the power it undoubtedly has unless it awoke in the depths as well as on the surface of each personal consciousness an echo that could transcend it. Even more than the Confucian model that it suggests, this slogan identifies the individual with a social reality, and far from splitting or alienating his personality, provides him with a passionate enhancement of his own consciousness. The Party comes to polarize the collective consciousness towards a civilizing end.'

Systems, ideas and notions—'thought', the seventh heading in the list—enter belatedly into this dialectic, just in time to be apprehended by the 'whole' man, in that torrent of passions, in

28

the fullest sense of the word, which is the flow of history. As
Mao has told us: 'the strength of the peasant class is like that of
raging winds or torrential rain.'

One cannot fail to notice—and this is the philosophical
reference mentioned earlier—that this dialectic is the exact
opposite of that by which Hegel went from the abstract notion
(*Begriff*) to the complete 'event' which, for him, was the Prussian
State. We know too that Marx, while turning this dialectic to
account in his own method, rightly accused Hegel of 'walking
upside down', as he had endeavoured to base the world on ideas
rather than the other way about. China, in this case, may thus
legitimately claim—if the present book truly conveys the movement of her thought—that she satisfies the requirements of
Marxism in her own fashion. Thought in China is now becoming, or is becoming once again, instrumental to action.

But what is not always recognized in this famous controversy
is the historical, and as such limiting, background of the pre-
eminence that a revolutionary movement born in Europe,
unique in history and bearing the stamp of its origin, happened—
and could not but happen—to assign to economic factors,
finally analysed by Marx in terms of man's physical effort. This
disharmony, to speak the 'cosmic' language familiar to the
Chinese, appears historically as characteristic of dawning indus-
trialism in the 'black' regions of the Rhineland and Wales. It
was then no doubt at the root of many evils. But it was too
ambitious an enterprise, at a time when we knew so little of the
rest of the world, to try to extract from it a social cosmology,
as the author of the *Communist Manifesto* and *Das Kapital* sought
to do. This meant taking the anomaly for the rule, and its
specific cure for a panacea. China under Mao, a modern leader
but with the advantage of being in close harmony with the
deepest values of her culture, could not but be particularly aware
of such an extrapolation, if only by reason of what China, on her
own account, brings into the historical picture. Such conclusions
would take Marxist criticism back to Engels' opinion, towards
the end of his life, when he judged his own and Marx's work
more impartially. One should not divide the total human fact

in privileging economic factors, except for the provisional need of some particular situation.

But China's daring attempt to adjust herself to the human situation as it 'happens' to be now, without losing sight of her rich historical background, does not mean that she is bound to her past any more than France, for instance, would be to hers by the fact that Descartes, for all his boldness, happens to have cut in our cultural history the figure of a conformist. It is just a question of getting our landmarks in perspective. For the true problem fortunately remains ahead of us, and what opinions we may have of our past and present are only one of its elements.

The plain fact we have to concede, as Robert Guillain soberly remarks, is that Chinese Communism can never be destroyed by atomic bombs. Let us do our best—that is, our worst: out of the ruins and misery of China, what government would be reborn (and one might add, after what guerrilla warfare!) except, as Mao has also said, a new Communist government more revolutionary than ever?

This book of M. Geoffroy-Dechaume's, more perhaps than any other contribution, gives us the chance of grasping the crucial evidence in one respect, which is that we are facing less a revolution than a revulsive crisis. It is a great help that this should also have been recognized and repeatedly stated by a particularly well-situated and well-informed judge, the Secretrary-General of the United Nations, U Thant. It is our policy of global superiority, both economic and cultural, based on real —but now obsolete—elements of military superiority, which has finally made the whole of China rise up against us, refusing to renounce her birthright. We try to carry out that policy under what is commonly called the 'umbrella' of atomic superiority, which in fact rouses China's desire to contest and overcome it. M. Geoffroy-Dechaume regrets, he tells us, among many other cultural losses the disappearance of our proverbial sayings; are we then likely to forget that 'where there's a will there's a way'? The powerful synthetic character of the Chinese script, and the precedence we are here told that it always gives to action and to conformation in and for action rather than to abstract speculation, should be a timely warning of the momentum that threatens to be China's within thirty years—to paraphrase M. Guillain's suggestive title.

Let us then go back to our landmarks and China to hers. Who knows, when mutual understanding is achieved, if 'the other side' will not find as decisive help as we may ourselves in a Descartes reassessed in terms of a broader humanism? For there is no question on either side, of surrendering or demanding surrender, nor, on our side—tempting as this may seem—of playing off Peking against Moscow, or Moscow against Peking. What we need is a meeting-point that should not be the point of common disintegration; and for that end, we shall have first of all to find both each other and ourselves. Meanwhile, we must not expect our two gigantic opponents to solve our problems by making us a present of each other's Marxism. Let us moderate our demands, on both sides! When an acceptable conciliation is at last in sight, the only people to ask more, and much more, will be those who not only put no hope in conciliation but passionately reject it.

Preface

THIS is not a traveller's tale, still less an essay in doctrinal controversy. China, for all its remoteness, is neither a collection of oddities, nor a field for our experiments, nor some Martian entity to be observed with detachment. We must understand China and ourselves at the same time; there is no other way. In the words of the medieval poem:

> '. . . si est de nos:
> ne vos sans moi, ne moi sans vos!'[1]

(That's how it is with us: neither you without me, nor me without you.)

Our failure to understand the Chinese starts, in fact, with a failure to understand ourselves, to recognize what they see and what they reject in us and about us. Each grows more unyielding, while a contracting planet encircles and binds us closely together, each seeming a monster to the other, with no means of communication—a conflict that has spread as far afield as Africa.

Although they are addressed to an authentic Chinese recipient the letters that accompany the ensuing chapters give only half the picture. They would only acquire their full meaning if we had China's answer, and thus a comparison between our values and hers—the values of a human group numbering close on a thousand million.

In our attempt to understand China we should go back beyond the events of 1949—the seizure of power by the men of the Long March—and the succession of facts which since that date have marked the history of that vast country. There are enough

[1] *Lai du Chèvrefeuille* (Marie de France). Twelfth century.

33

books, articles and reports describing in great detail what is happening in China, and to these we refer the reader who wants figures, anecdotes, first-hand impressions and quick explanations.

The perplexity we feel at times when we consider the facts about China impels us to probe more deeply into their causes, seeking the aid of other disciplines than those of the reporter or the economist. Thus the historian, in such a case, needs all the resources of the sciences that deal with man and those of philosophy if he is to see things aright. Such an ambition can scarcely be fulfilled. From a long contact with China's reality, it is proposed here to sketch a line of action, after an inquiry into the conscious and unconscious motives which today animate China and ourselves.

If we must believe in order to act, especially in order to act effectively, a completely rational understanding of one's actions is scarcely possible. And yet belief is unquestionably necessary. Now, we have ceased to believe on some essential matters. We question ourselves about aid to underdeveloped countries, about progress, about development, civilization and peace . . . but our convictions grow blunted and our most disinterested gestures, for that very reason, are frustrated by their own inadequacy.

The explanation attempted here is only a beginning, a short cut, even if it endeavours to cling as closely as possible to the reflections of those thinkers and scholars who, each in his particular sphere, have grasped a certain truth and at the same time have measured the overwhelming task that a synthesis of our knowledge would be. History never was a science, and never will be; it has today at its disposal a whole battery of data, psychological, ethnological, sociological, archaeological, linguistic and economic, all of unquestionable value, from which nevertheless it seems incapable of extracting any general interpretation of the existing facts which is valid or even credible. It is thus evident that the sketch of a synthesis offered here cannot satisfy specialists, since it will make only partial, and therefore distorted, use of their researches. It may even offend reason itself, when this is not backed by intuition, which can never be confirmed.

34

It is thus a rash venture, but a necessary one, since the various aspects of reality—political, economic and human—move so fast that they threaten to outstrip one's efforts and reduce them to insignificance. If this essay then seeks to sketch what our knowledge and beliefs, taken all together, might suggest, it does not require any special knowledge of China in order to be understood; it is addressed to 'men of reason'.

Considering familiar facts in a new light, I shall study the techniques, the psychology, the art, thought and feelings of China to derive therefrom a view of history and the meaning of the revolt which is already stirring one third of the human race.

References to various authors will here form part of a study which, without circumscribing its subject, will seek to reach down to its innermost depths. The aim has been to sketch that subject, to set it out in some sort of order, and to draw attention to its capital importance. It has been found useful to divide each chapter into three parallel parts: the first suggests concrete problems with the aid of selected examples, the second proceeds to a basic analysis of these problems so as to ensure as solid a foundation as possible for the comparative method which has been followed. The ambition of this study being to initiate answers to the questions which nowadays grow ever more numerous, each chapter is followed by a letter intended to illustrate and resume ideas which abstraction would quickly render unreal. This involves the risk both of sentimentality and of repetitiveness, which may however have their own use. But the real reason for this correspondence, as I have said, is that T'ang-lin really exists. And so these letters seek to set the tone for a future exchange of feelings not only between ourselves and China, that latter-day Sparta, but with all those men throughout the world who are distressed, or infuriated, at not being understood!

Set against what is called the West, namely the civilization born in Europe, a vast entity comprising all its manifold variants and extensions, set against all the nations which, to a greater or less degree, represent the West today, China is different. To see this requires an effort. To look at ourselves, not from some distant star but from the Chinese capital, to seek Peking's point of view, is a challenge to us. So many people, seeing liberty threatened, judge only in terms of 'blocs' or summary ideologies; so many are convinced of the somewhat Asiatic character of the Russians—on the evidence of slanting eyes or Slav temperament —that it would seem absurd to them to base one's argument on the hypothesis that there may be several forms of totalitarian State control, or that the Russians are closer to ourselves than to the Chinese. And yet the attempt is worth making. For Peking's point of view, which holds good for so many men, implies a way of life. To see the 'Europe' that the Chinese see thus involves grouping together the Russians, the English, the French, the Americans, and all the other citizens of nations having different and even conflicting political régimes, without losing oneself amid nuances which are often only of relative interest to the Chinese, or which may escape them altogether. This 'Europe', this 'Western world', which will be bracketed together throughout this study so as to avoid involving them in the meshes of politics, extends at least from the Urals to the Pacific! It implies notions of liberty, democracy, welfare, religion, and a view of man and the world, quite as much as details of dress. The latter is worth noticing: Nehru wore a rose not as an Oxford aesthete might do, but because of the significance of flowers in India, as a powerful symbol. And the modern dress assumed by Chinese women bears a message worth deciphering.

It seems necessary therefore to endeavour to look at China and at ourselves through Chinese eyes, and thus to break free of the mutual incomprehension, of a dialogue between the deaf which threatens mankind today. This essay attempts to bring some awareness of what China is seeking: one of the crucial issues of our time.

Chapter One

REVOLUTION

1 - A revulsive crisis

IN the closing chapters of this book we shall explore the idea that a relationship exists between the spatial and spiritual aspects of a society, in other words that its dimensions, its area and its density determine certain features of its mentality. The discovery of the New World transformed the mind of Europe. This suggests that the conquest of sidereal space may have important consequences of a similar nature . . .

Let us consider the spatial aspect of China. In 1775 the Emperor Ch'ien-Lung, by subduing the Miao tribes of Szechwan province, completed the internal colonization of China at the very time when, in another sphere, her millenary programme was being achieved by the annexation of Mongolia, Tibet and Eastern Turkestan. The Chinese Empire then extended over more than two thousand five hundred miles from north to south and from east to west. These distances still seem considerable to us despite our present means of travelling, When journeys had to be made on foot and on horseback, they must have seemed infinite. The court of Peking nevertheless maintained regular relations with the most distant provinces and kingdoms, and received tribute from them.

As well as this spatial vastness, consider the volume and density of China's population: demographic statistics, whose use Europe discovered only much later, were established in China even before our own era with a precision which guarantees their trustworthiness. We know thus that Chang-An, the capital of China in the 8th century, had two million inhabitants; that Hangchow, its capital in the 13th, had one million. Both these cities were thus in their day the largest towns in the world.

(Rome, at the apogee of the Empire, had one million inhabitants.) Thus at the moment when the Chinese Empire reached its greatest dimensions, in the 18th century, it comprised 200 million inhabitants and a string of huge towns. Great cities, it has been noticed, play a desacralizing, secularizing role. This influence becomes more marked when the increase of their population gives rise to those mass phenomena which Ortega y Gasset[1] has described as 'the new and formidable fact' of our own period in the 'West'.

The vast area, the huge population and their great cities may in part be held responsible for certain characteristics of Chinese society as we observe it in the 19th century: the sclerosis of the arts, of thought and institutions, the irreligion, the scepticism, the recession of virtues and beliefs. During the course of the last two centuries China has undoubtedly felt the psychological effect of this mass character the more sharply while, on the one hand, her population increased—to a figure of 650 million today —and on the other her vast spaces were constricted as a result of the progress of communications. This involved densification at the same time as increasingly numerous relations with the outside world and what has been justly called the impact of the West.

The Chinese Revolution may thus be explained by purely internal causes, by what might be called 'psychical geography', as well as by external causes. One would hesitate to draw a parallel between this revolution and earlier Chinese crises, did it not seem necessary, in order to understand an event of this magnitude, to refer as much as possible to the history of which we have direct knowledge. We may therefore look back to two great upheavals which China experienced during the 19th century: first the Taiping revolt (1840–1863) and then the Boxer rising (1900). Both had the same complex politico-religious character, mingling fervour with fanaticism in a wave of patriotism directed internally against the dynasty, and externally against Europe.

The history of China is not yet clearly understood, for it is based to a large extent on official annals which are difficult to interpret owing to the annalists' tendency to divide things into

[1] Ortega y Gasset, *The Revolt of the Masses*. Allen & Unwin, 1951.

rigid and symmetrical compartments. During the course of centuries, dynasties followed one another. Popular risings, born of various forms of discontent and promoted by secret societies, often brought to power a ruler of obscure origins, whose chief merit lay in giving new life to the Imperial principle and the mandate with which he and his descendants were invested by Heaven. Such was the process in which China, in the last century, seems to have been involved.

The Manchu emperors who first held power in 1644 did indeed impose a foreign aristocracy, but in the course of two centuries it took on Chinese characteristics to a large extent. True, its genealogies, grouped in clans and under 'banners', the unbound feet of Manchu women and the absence of pigtails (obligatory for the Chinese) among Manchu men, recall the origin of the ruling class. But Manchuria, under this same dynasty, became a Chinese province and, moreover, the new administration adapted itself to the old without noticeably altering it.

After a series of ten rulers, of whom K'ang-hsi and Ch'ien-lung represent the glorious and 'enlightened' apogee, the celestial mandate of the Ch'ing dynasty seems to have exhausted itself, and the time was ripe for one of those purifications which China's historic consciousness tends to introduce into the traditional cycle. Our closer knowledge of the administration and intrigues of the Imperial court between 1840 and 1900 leaves us in no doubt that the country, as a whole, had itself become aware of the vices of the régime and had so interpreted them that its discontent provided the impulse necessary for a dynastic transfer. If then the Taipings and Boxers attacked the Manchu dynasty, it was because it seemed indeed to have exhausted its celestial mandate. Was this the only cause? Or was there something else—a sort of 'revolt of the masses' accompanied, in the overpopulated centres of the vast empire, by a weakening of morale like that to which, among other things, the Roman Empire had succumbed? It is all the harder to tell because, at the same period, an external element interfered to confuse the issue: Europe began to penetrate China in every sphere. This Western wind fanned the inner unease, deflected the impulse and almost extinguished it through crushing military defeats. The fire smouldered, then flared out afresh, with a general force sufficient to involve the whole edifice in the revolution from which contemporary China has issued.

The complex character of the Taiping and Boxer risings deserves some attention.

In 1850 Hung Hsiu-ch'uan, chief of the 'long-haired' rebels,[1] raised the standard of rebellion, which spread gradually from the province of Kwangsi to that of Hunan, then to the whole Yang-tse valley, to Chihli, to Shantung, and finally affected the whole empire. For fifteen years civil war raged. The rebels occupied some hundred cities, but eventually, during the siege and later the capture of Nanking, which was their capital for three years, both their chief and his son, the 'heir apparent', committed suicide. This battle cost the rebels 'a hundred thousand dead'; every prisoner had his left ear cut off; a dynasty was still-born. But Europe had contributed directly to this result. It had taken up the defence of the old dynasty which, being moribund, was inoffensive; it had provided 'military observers'.

An eminent historian tells us how one of them, the young English Captain Gordon, promoted to General for the occasion, triumphed, by means of his 'Victorian' virtues, over that mystic revolutionary Hung Hsiu-ch'uan, who had almost succeeded in mounting the Imperial throne. Hung Hsiu-ch'uan's mission, Lytton Strachey says,[2] 'was to root out demons and Manchus from the face of the earth and to establish *T'ai-ping*, the reign of eternal peace. In the meantime, retiring into the depths of his palace, he left the further conduct of earthly operations to his lieutenants . . . while he himself, surrounded by thirty wives and one hundred concubines, devoted his energies to the spiritual side of his mission.' The temptation to be witty is irresistible. But in order to understand the event, there should perhaps have been less stress laid on certain customs which, though differing from

[1] So called because they refused to plait their hair, as a sign of protest against the custom imposed by the Manchus.

[2] Lytton Strachey, *Eminent Victorians*, 1918.

our own, were traditional—which greatly reduces their significance in this connection. The essential fact was that this revolt,
while fitting in with the usual pattern of a change of dynasty,
sought at the same time to attain a religious syncretism.

For the rebel chief claimed to be the brother of Christ. His
patriotic mysticism, thus coloured by a foreign religion, clearly
reflects the influence of European missionaries in China. It also
expresses a wish, conscious or unconscious, to absorb Christianity, to make it Chinese and thus to overcome it. A waste of
effort! During the years that followed, the internal disorders of
the country were intensified, while its external history was
marked by a series of military defeats, an expansion of foreign
missionary zeal and the rapid growth of commercial relations.

These developments helped to strengthen and indeed to
exacerbate the same tendencies at the time of the Boxer rising.
We recognize here a similar mystique. China in 1900, irrevocably
implicated in world affairs, sought to carry on her revolution
on two planes, spiritual and political, and on two fronts, internal
and external. The dynasty was weaker now, while foreign
influence had increased. A society of gymnasts, originating in
the villages of Shantung and named 'Plum-blossom Fists',
affiliated itself to the 'Society of the Red Lamp' and then to the
'White Lotus' sect. A whole network of more or less secret
societies, whose names suggest their Taoist or Buddhist character,
gradually organized the movement which was to become
known in Chinese history as the 'Volunteers of Patriotic Peace'.
These were the 'Boxers'. At first they organized processions to
stir up the crowd against the foreigner. The religious issue was
prominent from the first: a Buddhist monk incited the crowd
to set fire to a chapel, then to the homes of Christians, and finally
the massacre of missionaries called forth the armed intervention
of the Powers. The Empress Tze-hsi, then Regent, ordered the
initial disturbances to be severely repressed; she soon lost control
of the situation. A xenophobia of popular origin eventually
affected the élite; however, one of the Boxer leaders claimed
descent from the Ming Emperors (the preceding dynasty),
which implies that the movement was also directed against the

throne. Until the dramatic siege of the Peking legations, the Empress wavered continually in her attitude towards the Boxers, desperately attempting to deflect against the foreigner that which threatened herself: a wave of popular feeling, irresistible and blind to the point of suicide. At the turn of the century China lay prostrate under the heel of eight foreign armies, in alliance against her.

In the course of the ensuing analysis we shall repeatedly note that in order to overcome that twofold doom which has maintained an increasingly paralysing grip on her, China has recently undergone not only a revolution in the commonly accepted sense of the word, but a revulsive crisis. It may be compared to the violent and radical upheaval that deranges all aspects of an entire organism, with all its living forces, when it is threatened by annihilation.

To emphasize this let us imagine Europe, at the time when the first symptoms of its revolution—in France particularly—were taking shape, subjected to gradual infiltration by Islam, then suddenly attacked and vanquished, its major ports occupied and administered by active Muslim merchants. Would not our democratic revolution then have assumed quite another character? Would it have been concerned only with liberty and the rights of man? Would not France and Europe have turned, rather—at that period or later—to the deepest roots of their own being, looking beyond political and social reforms to discover, after some analogous upheaval, the true nature of nations, the price of our civilization?

Present-day China displays above all the twofold urge to achieve inner order and to limit, or assimilate, foreign influence. Such were also her aims—conscious or not—in 1860 and 1900. True, the Imperial system has disappeared; true, Communism is a new and essential factor. But the same patriotism, exasperated at the twofold danger from within and from without, still animates China, and we may wonder whether she has not become Communist in order to surmount Western Communism, as in a previous age she sought to adapt Christianity, in her own fashion.

Has not Mao Tse-tung recently predicted that 'the day will come when Marx, Lenin and Engels will appear slightly ridiculous'?[1]

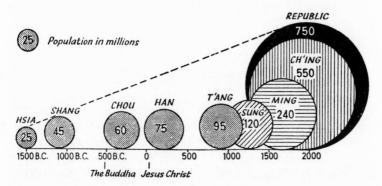

The more famous dynasties are represented here in terms of population. Although tentative (except for the present day), the figures are fairly reliable since they are based on censuses—long used for taxation purposes.

[1] Interview with Edgar Snow, 1965.

2 - The world picture

THE Chinese Revolution, the first symptoms of which, as we have seen, go back at least two centuries, developed amid a darkness which we took to imply decadence. Today it is emerging from its dawn and, little by little, taking its place in history. It is also breaking away from the Russian Revolution which inspired it, so that it has been thought to represent a permanent schism in the Communist world. If this were the case, in view of the vast masses mobilized, this Revolution would involve the whole of man and the whole of mankind. The influence of the Chinese People's Republic, particularly on countries with poorly developed economies, deserves a searching study.

The rise of democracy since 1789, and that of Socialism since 1848, in all their forms—liberal, planned or State-controlled—was accompanied throughout the world by a slow moral evolution which in China, in 1949, suddenly assumed, with great moral fervour, a totalitarian form. This State does not merely impose conformity of behaviour, which is the prime foundation of tyrannies, monarchies and dictatorships; it demands conformity of feeling, or the total conversion of the citizen. It has developed a mystique which goes beyond the requirements of the political and economic order; in what respect, we shall attempt to discover.

The most immediate aspect of this Revolution is that of an ancient and complex civilization seeking to adjust itself to the present, and to that end setting itself up as a modern state. China, centralized once again, is playing a part in world affairs. During the latter days of her Imperial unity, at the beginning of this century, China had no Ministry of Foreign Affairs nor even a flag of her own. Today she boasts all the attributes of an international power—to which her size alone would entitle her —and the influence due to her originality.

After fifteen years of this régime, one is tempted to speak of a mutation, of a China unrelated to her own past. But outside the sphere of ideology, what has happened to the ordinary Chinese man? Mental attitudes are extremely persistent, if still inadequately understood; they obstruct the efforts of zealous idealists in every land. Human nature defies human intentions, and controls things in its own way. Despite fifty years of constraint, the Russian, for instance, remains much what he always was, and diversity throughout the world seeks thus to assert itself.

China was never conquered, or else she successfully assimilated her conquerors. The semi-colonial state often referred to consisted of a commercial régime, with 'unequal treaties', harbour concessions—insignificant in comparison with its vast territory or with the extensive colonies of classic type—side by side with the growing ascendancy of the 'West'. If the Powers, at the height of their political expansion, resorted to these unusual methods to penetrate into China, it was less on account of their national rivalries than because the obstacle to their ventures was of a peculiar nature. Trojan horses were needed to penetrate within the besieged Empire. One such was Shanghai, from which the effluvia of a foreign civilization poured into the Chinese interior. That time is over.

China has closed her doors,[1] retiring within herself as though wholly concerned with sifting out what suits her from what repels her. This can be accounted for by her will to choose between all the foreign elements that press upon her, and that had at one time invaded her in insidious confusion, threatening her with a cultural and moral mutation. This choice had been imperative, no doubt, ever since the first contacts between China and 'Europe'. It had dictated a series of reforms, but these invariably lagged behind events. Each of them, no sooner realized,

[1] In 1964 there were apparently only 500 foreigners resident in China for any length of time: less than one per million inhabitants!

made others necessary; an apparently ineluctable sequence of cause and effect transformed the political system, the economic and social structure, the very nature of Chinese society and even its mental attitude. The danger of such an invasion had been foreseen by Japan when, for two whole centuries, she kept Europeans out of her archipelago, before once again welcoming them freely. But we should seek in vain a parallel between China and Japan; the latter, despite the originality of her culture, has succeeded with characteristic virtuosity in adapting borrowed elements to her own style with apparent ease. Nothing of the sort happened in China, for here foreign influence affects *the civilizing centre of the entire Far East*. This centre, this cradle was already in a state of crisis when a profusion of 'European' factors invaded it, intensifying its confusion and provoking the radical upheaval that is the present revolution.

Whatever China today takes from outside, she undoes and refashions in her own way, as the Romans of old pulled Chinese silk to shreds and wove it afresh into fine gauze for their ladies.

At certain periods China was divided into as many as sixteen different kingdoms. Unified today, she forms the centre of a Chinese world extending over the whole of the Far East. We must take into account the past of this political and cultural metropolis, as well as what it is in process of becoming. Its Revolution combines certain features of what, in our world, made up the Roman Empire, the Middle Ages, the Renaissance and more recent epochs. The Chinese order imposed itself on neighbouring lands: Tibet, Mongolia, Manchuria, Korea, Vietnam. Like 'Europe', China displays a diversity of spoken languages—described as dialects—but she enjoys the use of an international medium, the written language, a powerful unifying factor like our own Medieval Latin. As in seventeenth century Europe, manual skill and the mechanical arts, coming into high esteem, have overthrown scholastic thought and brought science into the front rank, with unforeseeable consequences.

But, it is said, history has now entered on its universal phase; it is no longer possible, as it once was, to consider it in terms of different civilizations. It includes the whole human race. This point of view, common today, tends to underestimate the breadth, density and nature of the concepts of culture and civilization, to reject Spengler and Toynbee in favour of a dangerously simplified conclusion. No doubt we are more keenly aware than in the past of the universal nature of man. But should we on that account forget the characteristic reality of each society, derived from the antiquity, the continuity, the common nature of its heritage? Should we refuse to allow a special destiny to that great complex whole that is China, and reduce it to the nineteenth-century European definition of nationhood, pinning our faith meanwhile to an evolution to which by an instinctive and sometimes justified pride we attribute the direction that is easiest and most favourable to ourselves?

'Western civilization appears to be the most advanced expression of the evolution of human societies, but things are by no means as simple as that . . .'[1]

Contemporary life impels us to consider broader forms of human solidarity than those of nationhood. These, too, we find in China. The unity of her world is both temporal and spiritual. A great complex civilization, once divided into warring kingdoms, has newly established internal peace and a political and moral order. Her entry on to the international scene poses problems whose difficulty increases according to their economic, political and psychological nature. To define the most basic of these involves a glimpse of a multiform reality which is often difficult to grasp. China being unified, her political role is not bound up with her economic power. Even the marginal products of this immense if 'under-developed' country already play a considerable role in the world market. But her influence, furthered by this economic action which is still in its initial stages, belongs to an ancient continent-wide tradition which had been temporarily interrupted. This explains her diplomatic activity —surprising in view of her vast internal difficulties—which might seem ambitious or excessive. But China does not merely wish to recover her historic suzerainty. She seeks to play her

[1] Claude Lévi-Strauss, *Anthropologie Structurale*. Plon, 1963.

part in world affairs. Already in Asia she is once more the point of equilibrium, ruling with apparent ease in an atmosphere that is congenial to her policy, but her actions have a universal bearing. It seems then, at a time when peace must be established less by force and more by a gradual adjustment of values and quantities, that the outside world will have to concede to China the role that is her due, and for which she is so keenly striving.

The sheer magnitude of the Chinese experiment would account for the influence it naturally exerts over nations which are not ready to adopt 'European' formulae outright. Signs of this influence are already observable. On all sides, the nations are looking towards this Power, so old and yet quite new, which inspires alternately hope, sympathy and anxiety. Diplomats consult one another, delegates and partisans measure their strength. A tense situation has arisen, centring round the giant. The problem is a new one, for during the last period of Imperial China (the Ch'ing dynasty, 1644–1912) the difficulty of communications resulted in the Western nations' failure to take China seriously or to understand her: an attitude which is out of the question now.

China is a civilizing centre on a world scale, and at the same time a State. The result of this dual character is that China's position does not merely set problems of foreign politics. It demands a two-way adaptation. China is changing and the world is going to change. We may well see, for instance, Chinese methods of government or administration being adapted to non-European populations and offering solutions to that pressing and perplexing contemporary problem, the application of certain forms of democracy to societies that are not ripe for them. China can provide original methods of dealing with the over-population that threatens certain countries, and which she has already experienced. Chinese institutions will have to be examined. And is it out of the question that they might suggest new ideas to 'European' civilization itself?

In the past, China has already played such a part. In the 18th century, awareness of a Chinese order, although inadequately known and understood, stirred profound currents of thought and feeling and played a considerable part in our own development. It is said that Vauban's *Projet de Dîme Royale*[1] and Fénelon's *Lettre au Roi*[2] took their inspiration from China. Her influence is also seen in the theory of enlightened despotism, the philosophy of the Physiocrats, and in our own Civil Service competitions[3]—'careers open to men of talent'. Oriental ideas

[1] 'Vauban, seeking to justify the principle of the new tax he proposed to institute, the *dîme royale*, which was an income tax from which nobody was to be exempt, replacing the *taille*, a personal tax restricted to a certain category of citizens, felt it necessary, to justify his proposal, to show that it was no innovation since (among others) 'the King of China also makes use of it throughout his empire' . . . . The population problem was consequently one of Vauban's chief preoccupations. But to assist repopulation two essential things were necessary which were unknown in France in the 18th century: the exact state of the population of the kingdom, and the laws governing population increase. 'We must have an exact census of the present population.' Here the example of China showed Vauban that his idea was not Utopian, since the Chinese government had been able to establish statistics on its population, which consisted at the time of '58,550,051 souls, not counting women, infants, soldiers, magistrates, eunuchs, persons of royal blood and schoolchildren, which would bring the total population of the Empire to 100 million at least' (in fact over 200 million).' Virgile Pinot, *La Chine et la formation de l'ésprit philosophique en France*, 1640–1740.

[2] It is uncertain whether Fénelon's letter actually reached Louis XIV. Written in 1694, it makes no direct reference to China, but the fact of addressing such an admonition to the sovereign was sufficiently unprecedented in Europe, and coincides too closely with the time when, thanks to the Jesuits, men's thoughts had turned to China, for us to consider it as mere coincidence. Since the earliest days China's fundamental political principle had been government by a king under guidance from wise men, who influenced him by means of similar 'remonstrances'; these, from feudal times, had formed a strict part of the vassal's duty, and as such have played an important part in Chinese history.

[3] The first examinations were instituted in China in 165 B.C. In 622 the foundations were laid for regional and metropolitan competitions open to all. By 1066, they were held every three years in the capital. From 1370 onward, the system included three types of competition (district, prefecture, capital city), corresponding to the French *baccalauréat*, *licence*, and *agrégation* examinations. This system, which lasted until 1905, formed the basis for a 'Civil Service' whose merits were praised by Montesquieu, Diderot and Adam Smith. In 1835 an Englishman wrote that this Chinese invention might, like gunpowder and the printing press, change Europe. The Civil Service was established in England in 1855 after being tried out in India, and in consequence of a report asked for by Gladstone; there had been a sharp debate in the House of Commons between the upholders and opponents of the 'Chinese principle'. This is, essentially, the replacement of the venality of official posts by an efficient hierarchy of permanent functionaries, recruited according to merit by competitions open to all,

thus borrowed from a remote Empire whose majesty, institutions, political and social stability were recognized as far afield as Europe, contributed in no small degree, through the medium of the French 'Philosophes', to the overthrow of absolute monarchies. Today, the Revolution that has overthrown that Chinese order involves all human societies and has set, since we are ourselves in the throes of a grave moral crisis, an authentically ontological problem.

Faced with the complete cohesion and the general mobilization of a whole section of humanity, one's imagination falters. Trying to grasp the panorama, we catch only fragments of a truth which is human indeed, but unfamiliar. It defies our reason. China is making a clean sweep of part of her own past as though to see things more clearly, and she gives us mental encouragement to do likewise. It is not so much her great size that makes such an effort necessary—as though one had a huge and over-active neighbour who could not be ignored and with whom one must come to terms—as the feeling of the experiment being attempted today by a civilization besieged and beleaguered, with its back to the wall, and inspired by a sort of vengeful desperation.

And yet one dare no longer speak of 'eternal China' for fear of provoking smiles or irritating certain impenitent rationalists, athirst for abstractions and intellectual victories. It is the nature of revolutions to obey certain rhythms. And we may wonder whether Russians and Chinese are not today arguing over points of doctrine which experience has already left far behind. Within the ocean of time, history moves at different levels—from the ripples or billows on its surface to the imperturbable

before a permanent jury. In France, competitions were established successively for each branch of the Administration: in 1869 for the Cour des Comptes, in 1872 for the Conseil d'Etat. In 1899 the *Statut de la fonction publique* was passed, and thenceforward competition became the normal method of selection for candidates for permanent posts. It may therefore be presumed, although it is difficult to prove, that this system, unknown to Egypt, Greece or Rome, was at least partly inspired by China.

deep-sea swells. The world's thirst for unity is so urgent today that it leads to an ambiguous and impatient demagogy. We want men to be like one another in all respects; and yet we think in terms of 'economic man' or 'Soviet man' or 'free man'. We refuse to recognize differences, and we grasp only a single denominator. One dare not make a general contrast on any single point between East and West. Now a civilization is a complex function, primarily psychological, and it stamps each individual with an unmistakeable imprint.

The Chinese Revolution forces us to face, in order to discard it, the prejudice which sees our own way of thought as a universal norm, and to seek a new understanding of the facts. Like the French Revolution, which even today forms the theme of many studies, the Chinese Revolution will be subjected to innumerable analyses. We, its contemporaries, attempting to grasp the event, cannot do so with detachment. For thought and passion are here intermingled. And the observation of facts—even if we had an ampler store of these—would not be enough. Life, at this level, requires a new kind of awareness.

Thus on either side of the frontiers of China and the 'Western' world a readjustment of truths will have to be made, willingly or unwillingly, and an interpretation will emerge. We must look deep into ourselves. Our science and our intellectual techniques appear to us supreme, for they ought unquestionably to enable us to deliver humanity from the material poverty which has been its lot from the beginning. But some philosophers have had the courage to say that science does not prevent our ignorance of reality from being absolute. The generous ideal of suppressing hunger throughout the world authorizes a form of action which is humanitarian but inadequate, for even if prosperity became general, the real, the great difficulties would subsist. And wherever we look, we find that contemporary science 'has no answer to give to the problems of our time'.[1] For China, science remains an instrument, an indispensable cultural contribution serving to convey a moral exaltation that corresponds to some transcendent aim.

[1] Brunetière, *Questions actuelles*, 1907.

Faced with the widespread levelling of standards of living, China's instinctive struggle, like that of every other country, has been primarily to preserve certain values. In every land the old order is threatened by the breakdown of economic, social, political and psychological structures through the application of new techniques. We ourselves have not escaped this transformation. All the more reason for paying attention to the profound repercussions of the crisis that grips those societies in which the contrast is sharper, the conflict harder, between traditional culture and the new, massive contribution of alien techniques.

The Encyclical of 1961 tells us that respect for human values and for a moral order are indispensable for peace. And surely the threat to peace will be intensified by our failure to understand the values of China and its moral order, its nature and its methods of self-defence. There is a terrifying gap now between our knowledge of the physical world and our knowledge of mankind, between our material and our spiritual progress. Institutions and human relations are still ruled by instincts that spring from an ill-deciphered past. We sense that nations are barely emerging from obscure unconsciousness. What can we say about relations between civilizations when some of these, such as China, set themselves up as modern States? Is this not a theme for active reflection? Is not China that dynamic, that almost explosive reality, that 'critical mass' the continual bombardment of which by foreign particles threatens to provoke some world conflagration? . . . An inquiry into the nature and meaning of the Chinese Revolution thus seems as urgent for peace as all efforts towards development or disarmament.

3 - First letter

Dear T'ang-lin,

How many years is it now since we last met? What's the use of counting them? Are we not the playthings of our epoch? One day, international relations open up happy prospects for friendship; the next, they confine it within narrow paths, choked up with weeds, at the end of which, through some tenuous and implacable gunsight, we may perhaps catch sight of one another, but fail to recognize each other!

China—unknown, unrecognized, misunderstood, then recognized once more. Why cannot we escape from these vicissitudes? The silence between us, the effect of an event, a situation, and not of your neglect or mine, obsesses me.

I have decided to break it. I'm writing to you on the off-chance, to your old address—where you lived before the Revolution. But what was that Revolution? No mere short-lived episode within the precincts of a palace, of that I am well aware. And what if it were to herald the greatest event in the world's history? When would this be realized? But the friendship between us does not belong to the present time. Today, few can find or foster such a relationship. Hundreds of thousands of human beings would seek one another across invisible frontiers if they had the hope of communicating as we once did, and as I shall attempt to do again. Who has dared attempt it, or succeeded in doing so? For my part I refuse to submit to this evil spell. I want to seize once again the chance that brought us together in those bygone days when, free from all restraint, we experienced that reciprocity of minds without which friendship cannot exist.

A revolution divides us from that past. A revolution: what does that mean? Is it to be measured by bloodshed, by gibbets and guillotines, machine-gun fire, the execution of kings or tsars? Or else by its principles, its slogans, its words and hopes and its slowly fostered passions, suddenly breaking out and stamped with an irrevocable seal? The ills that ravaged China resisted all known remedies. Your last Emperor, ending his days in a humble retreat, has been elected to your Parliament; his death would have had no significance. As for yourself, you are now a citizen of the People's Republic of China . . . The world is growing narrower and more complicated. Nations seek to be united, without knowing exactly what they are. How strange it is! There stirs within me the feeling that I belong to a father-land as vast as your own, my own nation merely a province of it, and the horizon becomes blurred . . .

While the varied memories of a country or a town once visited fade from one's mind, their reality is somehow con-centrated in the recollection of the human beings one has known there. Thus for me you have imperceptibly become China, and my consciousness of China. During all these years I have mentally pursued the conversations we once held, and every happening in China has become, as it were, superimposed upon them, so that I have to write all this to you before we may have a chance to see one another again.

But are you still alive? How can I tell? Will these letters reach you? The post, in China, is a revered institution. It is said that once two warring Chinese armies called a truce to let the mes-senger bearing letters pass through. I am willing, then, to believe that through the ideological battles now raging these messages may reach you.

To see each other again! Confucius tells us, in the opening line of his *Lun yü*,

'*A friend come from afar, that is also a joy.*'

But even before that—his very opening words—he says,

'*To study, and practise what one has studied, day after day, that is also a satisfaction.*'

56

In these difficult times, study at least remains to both of us, and here I have sought to practise my study. May my efforts bring you hope, as they have brought it to me!

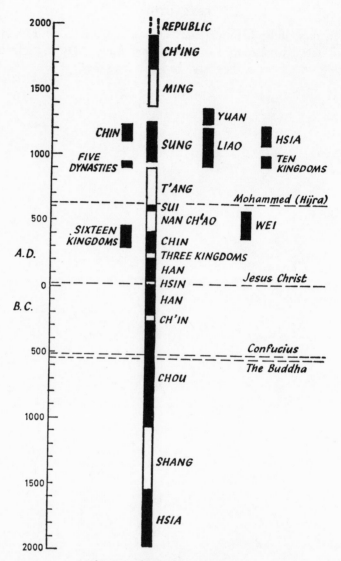

The Growth of China: Dynasties.

(The dynasty sequence reveals increasingly complex political situations. As Chinese territory expands, separate dynasties, states and capital cities sometimes exist simultaneously. There are also periods of unity initiated by great rulers.)

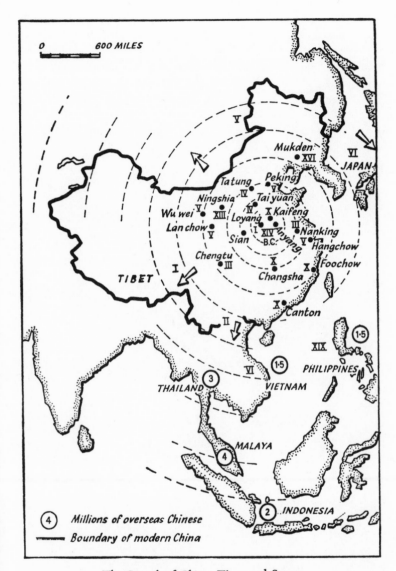

The Growth of China: Time and Space.

(Roman numerals refer to centuries when cities first became capitals, or when regions first came under Chinese influence. The dotted circles are to give an idea of the spreading of this influence around the cradle of Chinese civilization.)

Chapter Two

CHINA IN PERSPECTIVE

1 - *Magnetic writing*

THE 'European' who seeing, on a Japanese beach, some fishermen draw near, traces a Chinese character in the sand, soon finds himself the focus of smiling curiosity; he is forthwith admitted into a world which a minute before was closed to him, if not actually hostile. He is suddenly accepted on the strength of these few lines. Or if, in a Singapore restaurant, he spreads out a Chinese newspaper and starts to read it, an atmosphere of discreet interest, of whispered consultations, of slightly uneasy sympathy promptly tells him that his gesture has aroused the attention of the entire establishment.

Such is the position: in the present century, a difficult script, which unites nearly a thousand million human beings, sets between them and all the rest of mankind a barrier that is so considerable and so firmly established that the slightest breakthrough is noticeable and significant. For after curiosity has died away, a mysterious sense of solidarity lingers on.

Thus the peasants of Tonking, even today, display towards the foreigner who reads Chinese not only the respect traditionally paid to scholars in their ancient society but also a certain profound and active sympathy. They would be ready to stand by his side unreservedly on account of this kind of spell. It should here be pointed out that for a long time now the Chinese script has not been officially used in Vietnam. This country was however linked with China from the very dawn of its history as a remote province or a tributary kingdom. Its language gradually adapted itself to Chinese characters. In the course of centuries a Sino-Vietnamese literature—which had its great periods and its masterpieces—confirmed Chinese influence in the country. But

63

in the seventeenth century the phoneticized catechism was brought in by the Portuguese and in the nineteenth a national Latin script, the *Quoc Ngu*, definitely replaced Chinese writing in current as well as the official use. This involved political and psychological consequences the importance of which, far from diminishing, asserts itself defiantly even amid the troubles of the present day. The new writing had suddenly detached, one might even say severed, Vietnam from the Chinese trunk, while its educated class, thanks to the Latin alphabet, enjoyed ready access to Western thought. The change promptly assumed a political aspect, and was thus extended and confirmed. In a single century Chinese influence was dimmed in Vietnam, where there appears for the first time in history a symbiosis between the West and the Far East, between 'Europe' and China. For the latter persists everywhere, in spite of everything. This is the secret and the strength of Vietnam to which its intellectuals bear witness, as well as the peasants of Tonking.

It must be noted that the change of writing was not merely the transition from one alphabet to another; it involved more than a vague nostalgia for bygone days. The thing needs to be understood from within. Chinese characters, it is well-known, are both phonetic and symbolic. The change to Latin characters therefore involves not merely the transference of phonetic signs but the outright abandonment of symbols. Phonetic transference, or the simple conversion of one alphabet into another, already implies, it must be noticed, the loss of the etymology and aspect of words. What a strange blankness strikes us if instead of:

'*Bare ruin'd choirs where late the sweet birds sang*'[1]

we find the meagre shorthand equivalent: ⟍⟍, ⟍⟍⟍⟍⟍⟍

But a Chinese character, let us repeat, is often a symbol: like the Cross, which can be a Maltese cross, or a cross of St. Andrew, or a cross of Lorraine. . . . We do in fact meet in Chinese writing that hooked cross or swastika which, owing to Nazi Germany, has become the only Chinese character to be known, and hated,

[1] Shakespeare: *Sonnets*, LXXIII.

throughout the whole world.[1] To give up these symbols would correspond, in our society, to writing 'CROSS' or, worse still, its equivalent in shorthand, ⟶ , on wall or altar, instead of setting up a crucifix!

Obviously such signs, even though they have gone out of current use in Vietnam, still retain some of their power there; and where they are in current use, as in China or Japan, they maintain between the men who express themselves through them profound links of communion and solidarity.

Although they never connected the phenomenon with lightning, the men of our Classical antiquity noticed that amber (ἤλεκτρον) magnetizes particles of dust. The name of electricity was therefore given to the invisible fluid which was to bring brightness to our modern nights. The Chinese are magnetized by their writing, as though by amber. We, for the most part, observe only the modest side-effects of this attraction, without considering its power to let loose mighty storms or to bring light into the obscure walks of peace.

The ensuing pages will strive to show the particular virtue of this writing, which the Chinese set both in practice and symbolically at the very heart of their culture and civilization.

---

[1] Facing left, the hooked cross means the figure 10,000, or the heart of the Buddha; meaning ten thousand years it was the emblem of gravediggers who, throughout China, wore it until quite recently on their backs.

2 - Four civilizations

CIVILIZATION, as a whole, has become undefinable. It is spoken of, in the singular, as being human, worldwide, universal: scientific, technological or industrial: capitalist or socialist, Christian or Buddhist, urban or agricultural, rationalist or simply modern; and in the plural, civilizations may be traditional, 'different', primitive or indigenous, national or local, matriarchal or 'subjacent'.... We use the term at will to describe the whole or the part. Such a multiform reality defies analysis.

If one speaks of culture, confusion increases. All the epithets quoted above can be applied to culture; the word refers now to art and now to cookery. In different lands, and according to different schools, everything is intermingled. Scholars today even question our right to use the term. The point is purely academic, since it is increasingly employed in every country and has even become a basic form of action.

Thus, we have cultural relations, Ministries of Culture, and China in particular has her 'cultural revolution'. We must therefore accept it as a reality, even if it exists only in men's minds, for it is indeed an important contemporary force. Almost a century ago (1871) the Englishman Tylor defined culture as: 'that complex whole which includes knowledge, belief, art, morals, law, custom and any other capabilities and habits acquired by man as a member of a society . . .'

This it still valid, but is explains nothing. And neither the Fathers of Marxism, nor liberal psychologists, have succeeded in solving the mystery of the cultural differences that are everywhere in evidence. Since however we must strive to explain a concept which threatens today to lead men to kill one another, we might set forward the idea that culture is an organization of the human sensibility; in other words an organization at all levels of the relationships between man, endowed with certain somatic characteristics, and the world perceptible to his senses. And if indeed we are dealing here with what distinguishes man from the animals, may we not envisage culture as a relationship between the physical and the mental worlds, or else as mind projected into the social sphere? Summary as such a definition is, it seems justified by its heuristic value, and may help us to escape from the perplexity to which we are reduced today in such matters.

To return to civilization, that concept for which men have fought so bitterly during the course of history, which has inspired the deliberate sacrifice of millions of lives as well as the performance of innumerable disinterested actions, a fresh effort must be made to explain it now that the notion of 'different civilizations' has come to play a new part in human relations as China emerges, an immense political force, inseparable from its civilization.

Several recent writers have conceived of civilization less as an entity than as an organizational function of culture, thanks to three media which are: (1) writing, (2) the city, (3) specialized techniques.

Obviously this view is a schematic one. Civilizations have existed which lacked writing—the Incas for instance—and others which have had no cities, and it is a delicate matter to establish any strict distinction between civilized and non-civilized cultures. Wherever man exists, social functions no doubt obey identical laws. Similarly, within any great civilization, the proliferation and survival of cultures and their variants and their countless interconnections preclude any clear-cut division. One might describe the civilizing function as a metaphysical one, since in fact it transcends the social group and the political order which is that group's concrete expression.

We may thus examine how this civilizing function works, by means of writing, the city, and various techniques.

WRITING. This fixes language and thought. Writing thus makes possible the transmission and enrichment of the spiritual heritage through the course of ages. Without writing there can be little history; without it, memories are exhausted within a century, or three generations; without it no long-distance organization, no enduring laws are possible, there can be no continuous progress. Through language, to which it gives material form, writing remains closely linked to the biological factors of which it is, as it were, the projection. The thought and culture which it sanctions spread by its means and gradually cover the whole area which is being civilized. Indeed, the emergence of writing may be said to represent, in the evolution of humanity, a threshold of consciousness comparable to the genetic mutation which gave rise to *homo sapiens*. We witness the appearance of this invention in many parts of the globe without being able to ascribe a definite origin or origins to it, any more than to the various races of mankind. Phoenician writing, which absorbed Egyptian elements, spread throughout the world supplanting cuneiform and hieroglyphic scripts and producing the Greek, Roman, Arabic and Sanskrit alphabets, but it failed to penetrate China!

THE CITY. Etymology alone is enough to indicate the central role played by the city in this civilizing process. It is, primarily, a considerable grouping of human beings in a fixed spot. Here, a social role is imposed upon the individual in a special, diffused manner; a general agreement is gradually reached between individual and collective aspirations, 'communication' between individuals is established no longer directly on a personal basis but with the help of codes and intermediaries of every sort. A way of life and a political organization thus emerge, given concrete expression by the arrangement and shape of dwellings and monuments. The city is a melting-pot where disparate elements are fused to produce an alloy which if it prove strong, will be accepted and imitated; it is a swarming beehive whose patterns will be repeated throughout the civilized region. The layout of prehistoric or ancient towns reflects the sum of dreams and hopes that every town represents, the will to organize, to legislate, to administrate, the impulsion of faith and creativity. Types intermingle, dwellings are obliterated, but the monuments stand and speak to us. The Roman city was slow to take definite shape. Its markets having vanished, one must guess at their aspect, probably somewhat like our own. Similarly Persian bazaars and Chinese cities, laid out around the mosque and the temple, give us a hint of what life was like at the dawn of those other great civilizations.

TECHNIQUES. By this must be understood a whole set of differentiated techniques, not only material but also human: social (in other words, institutions) and spiritual (that is, at the apex, religions, or shall we say rituals). One might consider the whole as forming a complete technology which, as it improves, involves the specialization and differentiation of individuals, and consequently their grouping into functional classes and occupations, producing, according to circumstances, various structures and institutions the most successful of which became models to be imitated. These spread, thanks to the success of those inventions and experiments which leave their mark on each evolutive stage of civilization.

Thus without this threefold foundation of writing, cities and diversified techniques, there would be no civilization. Without this 'tripod', culture would glow but faintly. When on the contrary these three factors are present and firmly established, confirming one another, we have all the conditions for the existence of a psychic and cultural milieu of peculiar stability, capable of shedding its influence afar. History describes the successes and vicissitudes of civilizations all of which, according to some, are doomed sooner or later to extinction. Yet all the civilizations alive today have their origin in four regions of the world: Europe, Western Asia, India and China. Starting from these points, four great original cultural traditions, of comparable power and permanence, mingle their numerous and subtle variants in our world today.

69

Firmly established on these four bases of Attic marble, Babylonian brick, Indian sandstone and Chinese bronze, these traditions make up all civilized life in our day, ceaselessly enveloping and organizing the countless diversity of cultures except for those of certain rare social groups, still isolated, that ethnographers are hastily studying before their destruction.

This point of view is valid if it induces awareness of the originality, the perennial nature and the vast scope of these four great civilizing streams. It is still too summary, for it may tend to obscure the fact that the most widely diverse cultural influences spread in every direction and from one world to another, so as to make civilizations extremely complex.

Since Sanskrit writing, for instance, is said to be indirectly derived from the Phoenician alphabet, one might be tempted to believe that India's civilization comes from Asia Minor, which is by no means proven. The direction of the writing is important: Sanskrit, having renounced its first formula, runs from left to right like our own alphabet, whereas Arabic, Hebrew, Chaldean, Persian, Syrian, Turkish and Tartar writing runs from right to left, thus suggesting a unity within Western Asia which is confirmed in other ways.

The genius of a civilization, then, does not lie in any single one of its factors, which may be borrowed from elsewhere; it lies in the originality of the whole. Forms of writing, types of city, techniques, all may be propagated separately, and so indeed may any race, or cultural trait—including that supreme one, a religion—without necessarily reproducing the civilization from which they derive. What is characteristic is the combination within a geographical area of the three fundamental factors in an original whole. We should therefore not describe civilizations as being Christian, Islamic, Brahmanic or Buddhist, but as belonging to Europe, Western Asia, India or China, to mention only these four great wholes, themselves already overlapping and split up, from which are derived all those regional, national and local syntheses whose complex interconnections—past, present and to come—are liable to confuse us.

Today, cultures and civilizations are intermixed to such an extent that we seem to be at the meeting-point of all the ages rather than at a single point in history. Everything confirms this impression. Language, for instance, that mystery which sums up all the rest: our languages, which have emerged from the darkness of ages, expressing the subtlest movements of the human mind, bear witness to immemorial progress and are the very essence of our societies: today they are to be seen everywhere intermingling, changing shape, gaining strength or growing weaker according to some vast process whose laws are unknown. Today four kinds of writing, Roman, Arabic, Sanskrit and Chinese confront one another, attack each other, defend themselves or reach agreement, while men search for a new conception of the universe. This is a meeting-point indeed, but not at a moment of time: spread over centuries rather, which indeed is but a brief interval in that vista of limitless evolution which some venture to envisage. The tensions and resentments between men born of too sudden, one might say unnatural, contacts will take a long time to disappear. The sum of our modern media for diffusing thought, for transporting goods and people, may be compared to some over-active fertilizer that threatens to exhaust the soil and weaken the plant. The relations between civilizations have been profoundly affected thereby. Thus 'Europe' and China, flung headlong into contact, still remain too remote from each other for one to predict a time when they will attain true mutual understanding. The rhythm of the movement escapes us; yet we can perceive an acceleration. Laws which we can guess at from certain of their effects suggest that a force is at work like that of water, a force which, imperceptible for a long time, will suddenly cause a river to change its course, will bring down a bank or provoke the catastrophic flooding of the plain.

We readily accept the notion that one civilization may be superimposed upon another. But we thus ignore the fact that each civilization constructs its 'inner milieu', whose tendency is towards concentration rather than dilation, and that the expansion of its influence is merely a consequence of this concentration. If we can still speak of a 'European' world, of a Chinese or an Indian world, that is to say of vast social aggregates possessing their own forms of writing, their own cities, their original techniques, it is because there undoubtedly exists a dynamic process by which each one's contributions are diffused or assimilated, a continuous concentration within the various original centres, which in their turn radiate influence. Such is the basic mechanism, from which China is not excluded; and no other civilization has been superimposed on China's. She appears on the contrary as the most homogeneous of the four great millenary parent stocks. She seems to seek concentration, and yet she also seeks to radiate influence. China invented her own form of writing, her own cities, her manifold techniques, and her originality is thus threefold and appropriates all foreign elements, subjecting even religions—Buddhism for instance, and Marxism in our own day—to radical transformations before making use of them in the cause of her own expansion.

China's writing, for thousands of years the backbone of her civilization and the ferment which gave it life, must be considered in contrast with the Roman alphabet. The latter strives today to spread gradually over the whole world, yet, as a universal vehicle, it remains split up into a considerable number of languages. The Chinese script on the contrary is interlinguistic. Close on a thousand million people will soon be able to communicate by its means, for Japan still retains access to it. We must hasten to point out that despite its apparent complexity Chinese writing does not condemn the majority of the population to ignorance, a notion current in the 'West' but completely contradicted by reality. Each written character being a word, and some of these being very simple, every Chinese knows enough of them to have access to ordinary concepts and to the leading symbols. Not everyone is a scholar, but nobody is illiterate, thanks to this script which is both learned and popular. And the idea that China will sooner or later be obliged to suppress her ideographical writing is merely the effect of a sort of 'Western' misoneism.

Chinese towns are, like our own, the mould in which a way of life takes shape. A sufficient proof of this is that where Chinese communities forgather within the heart of other societies, anywhere outside the Chinese world, they create not merely Chinese districts but Chinese towns; this token of vitality and of originality can be recognized not so much in their architecture as in that solidarity which, for example, once found material expression in the Chinese central telephone exchange in San Francisco.

As for Chinese techniques, they are so different from our own that we might be tempted to believe they no longer exist, whereas on the contrary in their ceaseless inventiveness they seem to achieve greater harmony between mind and matter than do our own.

These three fundamental factors of Chinese civilization are subject nowadays, no doubt, to considerable 'European' influence. It is easy to take argument from certain examples of 'romanized' writing, certain transformations in urban building and in industrial techniques. But is China's culture, the object and indeed the subject of her Revolution, jeopardized as a whole, in its essential energy? Nothing suggests that this is so. China on the contrary has a vast latent power of diffusion which has been insufficiently appreciated.

For many people, indeed, China is no more significant than any other country. For others, she is merely a stream of figures, a string of facts. Her vast human multitudes embarrass our thought. Nothing exists for us unless it can be counted and measured. Journalists chorus their amazement in face of Chinese achievements and difficulties. One of them looked out of his Peking window one day and seeing the sky full of kites exclaimed, 'This is all that's left of an ancient civilization, flying away into the blue sky!' Again, a quite recent work, *The Psychology of Nations*, fails to mention China. By an instinctive, tenacious mental process, we seek thus to turn over the page, averting our thoughts from the confused chapter that went before and ignoring the fact that an immense drama is being played out continuously in our own day.

Scholars are nevertheless striving today to observe and classify the causes of social upheavals. Their learning is well-founded; their respect for mankind is genuine; their researches are active and thorough. Yet they too often remain platonic. The ethnologist on the one hand and the historian on the other might reach agreement if, faced with the ineluctable march of time, they dared sink their differences and pool their knowledge. But how could they apply one or the other of their specialized disciplines to the whole of a great complex civilization? The problem baffles exact science, and divides scholars into those who, giving up all hope of understanding it, withdraw into their special field—regional, limited, exotic—and those who, deliberately ignoring the diversity of human cultures, construct their Tower of Babel, their abstract society or world civilization. For the former, Chinese values are too universal; for the latter, not universal enough.

Many of our thinkers belong to the second category. Overcome with a kind of nausea, they avert their eyes from China and take no further interest in her. Though they are concerned about the evolution of the world, they fail to take into account something that is before their eyes, and that is possibly the gravest crisis of civilization known to history. The gravest, because it activates masses whose size and cohesion are unprecedented, and because it takes place in hidden depths and is related to the very nature of consciousness. Can we, however, set any hopes on Chinese thought? We no longer know whether such a thing exists. The fact that there are millions of intellectuals in China and an Institute for Philosophic Research in Peking ought to encourage in this sphere—the only one through which we may achieve any profitable understanding of the crisis—the interest or the patience needed to bring about some exchange of ideas. Certain observers discern the signs that herald a storm, but they are tempted to wait for the dust to settle. Yet this would be too late.

There is a mistaken belief, still widespread, that Chinese civilization is decadent or stagnating. This originated over a hundred years ago. In those days, judgements were formed on purely political grounds. Pretexts were soon found for shouldering the 'white man's burden'. China was so recent a reality that we were unable to interpret facts in the light of her long, imperfectly known history; the corruptness of a single mandarin served to explain the apparent sclerosis of the administration, and to confirm that of Chinese art. And sinologists themselves, confronted with China's confusion, dared no longer believe in the efficiency of a thought and culture which would soon be of purely archaeological interest. Yet meanwhile China overflowed her frontiers, displaying a vitality which, though discreet, was imperturbable.

Today, Chinese civilization remains firmly established on both shores of the Pacific; it radiates far afield in 'diaspora' or through influence, settles in the heart of American cities and the remotest archipelagoes, touches Africa and already looks towards the Atlantic . . . The Chinese world is expanding.

We hear so much talk nowadays of progress and decline, of evolution and destiny, that nobody can fail to be aware of an intense movement in which the future seems to be taking shape. Are the forces involved obscure and instinctive ones, helplessly dependent on passion or on some catastrophic mistake? Is there a gradual adaptation of men's minds and wills? Is any compromise possible? How can one answer such questions! We must first tell ourselves that the chances of survival or happiness for men, now more than ever interdependent, are bound up with their sense of the universal, in other words of their knowledge, their consciousness of themselves and of others. We must undertake this investigation, not to satisfy curiosity nor by way of pastime, but from a sense of the vital need not to lose our way in the disturbingly profuse complexity of our time.

3 - Second letter

My dear T'ang-lin,

One winter's day in Peking, long ago, I had been to visit you. It was shortly after your marriage. You and your wife were still students, and you lived at the back of the University in a tiny room with paper windows, two iron beds, a small table covered with cheap lace and a coke stove that offered poor protection against the bitter cold. Your family were well off, even fairly rich (since they had that house in Canton), and I know that each of your brothers had, according to his means, contributed to your education and your travels, since you were the intellectual among them, representing their conscience and their hopes. And you did not betray their trust. Every penny was precious in the cause of education. The modesty of your home affected neither your serenity nor your thirst for knowledge. I was impressed by the organization and economy down to the merest detail of your life together, expressing the harmony you were creating; by your intense curiosity about everything, particularly about Europe; and by the respect you showed for the spirit of ancient traditions.

A long separation without news gives particular significance to this memory. I shall always treasure the picture of your mutual understanding, of your evident unity, of the perfect harmony between you. Marriage lies at the very centre of human affairs. Your marriage spoke to me of long centuries. It reminded me that in China there were many sages, and few unmarried people... You taught me to what extent it is possible to do without mechanical devices and material comfort, and that the civilized life is above all an inward matter: courage, patience, method, loyalty, strength of character and, above all, respect for one's given word, for thoughts inherited. In these virtues lay your strength, as it surely does still today.

Now, after this long blank interval, that afternoon I spent in your home seems to belong to no time, no place. Our separation seems to me the silent but impressive emblem of our time; politics indeed seem to guide our destiny, but actually the whole of history, in all its complexity, has been moving like an avalanche. What separates us is not, as might be supposed, a mere diplomatic game. In this long absence, whereas in a few hours an aeroplane might carry us towards one another, in these years of silence I am aware of something else.

China and the West are increasingly strange to one another; the time is past when our philosophers tried to understand your country! And yet an irresistible force, despite the gulf between us, impels our worlds towards one another.

Did you not feel this when you flung yourself—with such enthusiasm and with such success—into the study of our world? You learnt to know France, England, America, and yesterday perhaps Russia. Your gift for languages, your sense of history, your subtle mind had all been pressed into the service of an insatiable thirst, a passionate search for the things of the West. You had questioned yourself about our art, our institutions, our music, our religion . . .

You asked me one day where the name Europe came from. I told you that the daughter of a Phoenician king, abducted by Jupiter and brought by him into this part of the world, had given it her name. The myth reveals the origin of our civilization, and above all of our *writing*. It displays, too, our inveterate tendency to personification: we see Europe, Victory, Liberty, Truth, the Republic as beautiful women; Love has its statues, Time and Death visit us with hour-glass and scythe. Even God himself . . . Your country, on the other hand, has not even a proper name; it is for you merely 'the middle country', the country of the central civilization. It is not a woman in a helmet; there are—or were—no statues in your cities, no portrayals of Science or Melancholy, those austere ladies created by the European mind!

77

Since the long-ago days when we talked together, events have brought us face to face with many such contrasts. You are far off now; and I am far from China! You have grown more Chinese and I more European; and we are both seeking for the meaning and direction of our lives, the remedy for the obscure threats that surround us.

Here I notice a material development which is both reassuring and disquieting. The more sharply we are conscious of the inequality between rich and poor countries, the more our prosperity tends to deaden our sense of certain values. In your country, meanwhile, the strain of urgent need threatens to break the moorings that kept your old world safe in the harbour of its legendary wisdom. Here, we over-refine, we cultivate details, we organize our leisure, in a kind of thoughtless but no doubt necessary exuberance; in your country, desperate solutions cut into the very fabric of your life. I can guess at your sufferings and your efforts. They correspond to a grave crisis that we all know; but of what nature is it? This is what I shall examine in these letters. I shall consider less the political aspect, although the fate of nations hangs on it, less the economic aspect on which our livelihood depends, than the moral aspect, examining the issues that lie in those momentous scales where East is weighed against West.

How close our minds once were! We could then delight in finding analogies. Now the time of differences has come. If we try to understand these better, to respect them better, we may be warned of the danger of racist and demagogic tendencies; we shall be exhorted to consider man as a whole, without distinction of race or class, society or civilization. The attitude is a generous one. But are there not in fact between oneself and the Other always as many contrasts as resemblances? In order to act, must we not take into account that Other and his special characteristics? Must not our minds, for that very reason, strive towards agreement rather than identification?

I shall therefore speak to you about worlds, in the broadest sense of the term. Not that I wish to construct some theory, but because this has helped me to escape from the misleading political

78

and economic notions of our time. In order to be at one with you, I shall try to forget the many hostile shades and factions within that Europe which for you includes Russia and America too: all those regions from which our civilization derives. You are quite right. True, civilization means Pa-ta-shan-jen[1] or Michelangelo, it means pyramids or rockets; but it also means the way one dresses, prepares fruit or counts on one's fingers. You peel an apple in the opposite direction from us; you count by folding your fingers over your thumb, whereas we spread ours wide. Is it mere chance? In my view it betokens, rather, the power, permanence and extent of our societies. What we call our behaviour, our sensitivity, our education and mentality are the very fabric of our being, enriched through the course of long ages and at length irradiated by consciousness.

To know how all this has happened is a different matter. Is the secret a question of quality or of mass? Does universality result from natural virtues or from sheer numbers? These questions surge up, as our anguish grows. How can one answer them? Diversity is too valuable for one to dismiss certain civilizations as decadent. If mankind is not united—and it is far from being so—it is because men remain different and strongly, instinctively attached by some vital impulse to that which distinguishes them from each other. Are they not prepared to suffer and fight and even to die for this?

That is why I shall search out our most important and most enduring contrasts so as to discover the deepest motives of our lives, and by every possible means to avoid indifference or contempt; today, more than ever before!

The longer our separation lasts, the more I fear lest the Chinese, while adopting some of our techniques, may revert to attitudes which leave us Westerners little opportunity for an understanding. Until the 19th century, it is said, we knew China better than she knew us; then the reverse became true. But today I don't know what to say. We are all familiar with your Emperors' concept of the universe: their China was at the centre of everything, while under the canopy of heaven at the four

[1] Famous Chinese painter of the 17th century.

corners of the square universe dwelt the barbarians. The almost instinctive hostile reaction of your crowds to any over-active foreign influence leads me to presume that your minds, open for a while to the outside world, are today withdrawing in passionate self-searching, under the incessant pressure on the frontiers of your life.

The Chinese often show a fondness for noise, shouts and crowds, which we resent. They find therein comfort, a refuge against the bitter blast, against loneliness and that personal absolute to which they are little inclined. Do China's masses bring the Chinese a sense of solidarity and security? They would not bring us such anxiety did we not feel that by thus drifting slowly away, oblivious of others, China is in danger of losing that universality which was her glory and her secret, in which the best hopes for the future still lie.

As I end, my thoughts turn once again to your conjugal harmony. This was more than virtue or tradition, convention or romanticism; it was the very substance of your minds and hearts, a profound sense of two-in-one. Your harmony seemed to me to be inscribed within a cosmic order; it could, and must, contribute to order in the affairs of men. This brings to my mind what Lao Tse said when he came back from his journey to the beginning of the world,

'My mind is darkened by what I have learnt and cannot understand; my lips are closed and cannot speak. I shall none the less try to give you an idea of what I have seen; I saw the Yin, the principle of female energy, in all its motionless splendour; I saw the Yang, the principle of male energy, in all its ardent vigour. The motionless splendour rose from the earth; the ardent vigour blazed forth from the sky. The two interpenetrated and intermingled inextricably with one another, and from their union were born all the things of this world.'

We are told that old China no longer exists today, that everything has been swept away, obliterated . . . But these two characters, with which are associated all the ideas that compose the Tao, these two great characters Yin and Yang from which all things are born—are they no longer taught, are they too wiped out, forgotten, forbidden? No! On the contrary they have been simplified, are easier to understand, simpler to recognize, like the Sun and Moon in the sky. Surely you still say, as you used to, as you have always said, 'After the Yin comes the Yang'—as we might say, sunshine follows rain, or every cloud has a silver lining—not with that vaguely superstitious spirit that clings to our proverbs, but with a deep-rooted hope, come wind come weather? How can one help believing that these two opposites united, the basis of your supple dialectics, still serve your universe?

Simplified, too, is the character 'Li', which we can only translate by a long series of different words: ritual, courtesy, morality, ceremony, custom, manners, style, respect, correctness, modesty, virtue, all of these together! This cluster of human values, this pivot of the Chinese world, this unifying mortar can surely not be dust today!

And then, my friend, there is heaven itself; no need to simplify that character. Two horizontal bars, heaven and earth, and two curved lines represent Man. His head in heaven and his body standing firmly on earth. Are there anywhere else in the world four strokes that arouse such meditations? Celestial Empire, world under heaven, heavenly mandate!

All these symbols, like stars glittering in your ancient firmament, help us to understand the movement of modern China along the hard path she has traced out for herself. Surely they cannot have become suddenly dimmed and have ceased to guide your hopes, even in the privacy of your home, which tonight I recall so vividly?

> '*In life, in the days of our youth*
> *When we part we think we shall easily meet again.*
> *But today you and I are withered, growing old.*
> *And can no longer recall the farewell words we once spoke.*'[1]

[1] Shen Yüeh (A.D. 441-513)

Chapter Three

CHINA ENVISAGED

1 - The realm

In our effort to form a clear image of China, we are detained in and caught up by details which we tend to magnify. For instance, seeking to distinguish between the Chinese and the Japanese, we may perhaps refer to those voluminous black coiffures, lacquered and pierced through with long pins, the tradition of which still lingers among Japanese women. But this fashion, as T'ang statuettes bear witness, came from China over a thousand years ago, together with that of curved roofs over open pavilions. If we explore too far back we are liable to lose our way. But that risk must be taken. For China is to Japan as a park is to a garden. The latter could be taken in at a single glance, but for the variety of its flowers and the skill of its planning which continually entice and delight the eye; whereas China attracts us by its vast spaces, inviting us to leap into the saddle and gallop towards mountain tops or forests, through waste lands and rugged paths towards the undefined limits of its domain.

China's origins are infinitely complex. Already in the Stone Age, from Tibet to the Pacific, from the Mongolian steppes to Burma, there existed a vast area inhabited by sedentary, agricultural folk, who, as first bronze and then iron appeared, came to form distinct communities. Quite early on we find the little fatherland of Shang[1] established in the bend of the Yellow River, its people endowed with particular originality and vigour, and with the secret of acquiring civilization from others even while 'civilizing' them. It may be asked, is that such a secret, is it not the common characteristic of all nations? The fact remains that

[1] Or proto-Han.

the Chinese faculty for assimilation and expansion has always been exercised with singular success. The process has gone on unremittingly, in spite of the agitations of an eventful history, in spite of internal conflict and foreign invasion. *It is still powerfully at work.*

Our basic concept of China, then, must not only take in its urban masses, its peasantry rich with the secrets of a whole continent; it must take in China's function. Henceforward this function involves the whole world, for China still seeks to give out as much as she absorbs, having from her earliest days craved a sort of fundamental reciprocity in her relations with the world outside.

This explains how the Chinese conceive of foreign lands primarily as cultural realities, the only sort that counts in their eyes. The racial problem means less for them: from the earliest times, there has been so much inter-breeding in their country that they would never think of describing men as White, Red or Black . . . far less as Yellow.[1] Elementary reactions confirm this; the Chinese man in the street, if he sees a European, promptly asks his nationality. This general curiosity springs from a desire to place the foreigner in his right context.

One day when a Frenchman was standing on the city wall at Nanking, looking down at the famous lake, he was shyly accosted by two students. As they asked him the inevitable question, he told them to guess the answer. When they had exhausted the resources of their memories, he told them where he came from. Then one of them, turning to his companion, exclaimed, 'Oh yes, of course, France! Remember, the land of painters and scents!' As valid an image, surely, as that of a woman's hairstyles! What then is the image we form of China today?

[1] The concept of 'yellow' races appeared for the first time in seventeenth century Europe.

2 - *Prisms*

ROCOCO artists created an imaginary China made of silk, porce-lain and lacquer, a delicious and insubstantial dreamland. They associated China with Chinoiserie, with the language of the fan and of the minuet, with the 'Embarquement pour Cythère'.[1] We have not recovered from this. Our minds, ever prone to evasion, still indulge in these fancies. An aura of exoticism surrounds China to this day. And beyond China there is still the moon, which we actually plan to visit first!

The original creators of this eastern wonderland, Marco Polo and Mendez Pinto, as they embroidered their colourful tales, aimed at indulging the public taste for prodigies and thus arousing an interest in distant lands. Travellers from afar can tell what lies they please, for who is likely to put their stories to the test? Their descriptions, nevertheless, provide precious evidence. Much later, Europe sought to discover China. On New Year's Day, 1700, a great Chinese fête was held at Ver-sailles. The fashion took on, and the 18th century witnessed an undeniable Chinese influence. But there was no reciprocity. A dense curtain separated worlds between which no contact existed. Reality, glimpsed for a brief season, vanished once more. It reappeared at the time of the gunboats, steeped in literary exoticism and the reek of opium. Our poets and novelists, far from fulfilling their mission of giving artistic form to real life and thus interpreting it more truly, sought to amuse us with anecdotes and local colour. One painted melodramatic pictures whose interest was purely visual. Another made a system out of

[1] Watteau's famous painting is supposed to be influenced—as far as the dis-tant scenery is concerned—by Chinese landscape artists.

exoticism. Like Prometheus, he tore ideas, lines, whole sections from the sun of Chinese poetry, to build up his own ephemeral fame. He was not merely a plagiarist but a counterfeiter, misleading us and obscuring the truth. He sought to keep men alien and strange to one another; considering that 'diversity was on the decrease', he tried to foster it artificially.

Today we need the whole of China, and China needs the whole of 'Europe'. In other words, not facts alone but a sense of reality. How can this be attained save by multiplying whatever might further each side's awareness of the other?

We must reject the dilettante's attitude, 'China? Why, what a fascinating subject that must be!', and equally, that sort of eccentric specialization which puts the sinologist on a par with the astronomer. We must learn to control those feelings, those passions, that sentimentality that make us say ecstatically, 'I adore China and the Chinese,' or, with a frown, 'I dread and despise them.' To dissociate oneself as much from the sinophil as from the xenophobe, to strive towards a clear unbiased vision of that third of the human race, is for us an urgent necessity.

If it is undeniable that certain techniques have overrrun and unsettled our planet, destroying old traditions as though by fire, shattering cultures and making civilizations totter, how can we any longer indulge in complacent exoticism? Those who still do so lack a sense of their responsibility. They almost remind one of that versifying bomber-pilot who praised the beauty of the blossoms of dust that sprang up where his death-dealing projectiles fell. Involvement in the drama has become imperative; we must seek to look behind the setting of flowers and willow trees, beyond the scented darkness and the unfamiliar atmosphere, to reject what is merely strange, what strikes the eye. Poverty, hunger and above all hope must be reflected in our picture, and all those states of mind which can no longer be ignored. Life and death are at stake. The hour is past for indulging in romantic effusions.

Yet the temptation remains strong to linger over those countless ornaments with which China seems deliberately to surround herself. Her place-names suggest flowers, gold, jade and even headier images which, perceived from outside, cast a disguise over reality. The Peking Opera, though it goes round the world, is still misunderstood.

If we condemn literary exoticism, dare we then play at metaphysics, selecting esoteric fragments to bind them into mysterious wreaths? Religious thought when it is torn from its setting is like that luminous deep-sea fish which, brought to the surface, bursts like an empty sac. Any transcendent system needs to be treated with respect and caution, and to be considered in its right context, else instinctive laughter will shatter its fragile teguments. Some people take up Zen Buddhism out of intellectual snobbery, while they would be better employed saving their souls in a simpler way. But more commonly, Eastern religions are conceived of as a whole, to be more readily dismissed, Buddhism and Taoism being flung pell-mell into the junkroom; thus we lose sight of the universal value of their messages, their living reality in countless hearts.

In the same way we are fascinated in our leisure hours by 'curios'. The fashion for these is still very much alive. And while the expert eye or finger dwells delightedly on some carpet or figurine, some table or cup or screen, 'Chinese' remains a synonym for 'incomprehensible'.

Fortunately there exist other bridges than sensational literature, occult practices or yellowing ivories. There are museums— mirrors of art and mankind. A new awareness is coming to life in these today, for each of us can see himself reflected there through time and space. And China is at our side even in the everyday life of our own time: Chinese dresses, crockery and simple domestic objects can be bought in any store, while almond eyes are in vogue, perhaps through some frivolous sense of solidarity with a people whose rigorous destiny keeps it apart from the rest of mankind. And there is, or should be, photography, which attracts our attention on every side. The camera eye, indeed, has a vital part to play. Pictures, we are told, are supplanting books today as an instrument of civilization. Everywhere, photographic evidence compels recognition and conditions our thoughts. It mirrors reality, inviting one to observe and scrutinize, and pins one's gaze on some detail that enlarges the fleeting instant. But instead of the ten thousand photographs of China that we need, we get a mere handful! Just as from the Renaissance onward engravings served to arouse Europe's political and religious feelings, the conscience of Parliaments or the zeal of the Reformation, so today photographs could change men.

And then there is the cinema, which some day will discover its true mission. Even more than photography it can stir up every feeling, from the best to the worst. When Asiatic peasants behold on the great screen before them the ruin of a typhoon-ravaged harvest, a deep shudder runs through the entire audience. These fields of grain, scorched and flattened, are not a mere studio set; the real drama breaks forth. Too often, however, the drama is a false one, suggesting the still irresponsible childhood of this art. Too often aimless research is set at the service of futile or insignificant causes, exoticism or eroticism. The cinema carries into the furthest corners of foreign lands those examples of pointless violence, like children's warlike play, yet no longer innocent: false images, cultural aggressions, for which a heavy price must be paid! And all this intensifies the misunderstanding for which the cinema might nevertheless provide a powerful remedy.

There is always, too, the picture provided by travellers returning from China laden with notes, telling what they have seen and what they think of it. They are often men who have grasped some truth powerfully, whose penetrating or agile minds make them seem like well-trained athletes ready for any test. And in China such tests will be imposed on their common-sense, their logic, their very conception of existence; they rush into the arena ready to see everything, hear everything, take in everything. Unfortunately their course is soon slowed down; they are forced to follow a narrow path and submit to the official, the interpreter and the uncertain diagnosis of a many-sided and dazzling present. In any case, being anxious to speak to their public in the language of facts and figures which it likes to hear, they are constricted in all directions. How can we

reproach them for those tales of proletarian masses, yellow
peril or blue-clad ants, inevitably accompanied by that fateful
figure of 650 million?

And then one tends to emphasize the split between yesterday's
China and the People's China, to be influenced by that contemporary obsession, the contrast between two forms of democracy, State-controlled and liberal, both in fact of 'European'
invention. 'What needs to be realized', a true expert once said,
'is that China is a country where the birth-rate and the death-
rate are equally high'. This was true, at the time, of men as well
as of words, of ideas and institutions. Yes, China has changed.
For the moment it seems as though the flames of the Revolution
have consumed all that the ancient Empires had built up. We
see only red embers. Communism conceals China from us. Its
partisans indeed go so far as to say that this ideology has at last
delivered China from that thousand-year-old stagnation during
which a powerful mandarin class, prone to corruption and
exploitation, steeped in blind scholasticism, armed with esoteric
learning, ruled oppressively over an ignorant and superstitious
populace. They forget its religion, its philosophy, or see in these
merely 'opiums'. They deny the evidence of the peace that
reigned during the dynasties, of a social harmony that survived
a hundred revolutions and a thousand wars, of a vitality which
has constantly pervaded the entire community, of a genius
powerful enough to spread its influence over an empire which
was not static and rigid but constantly expanding, and which is
indeed in process of expansion at this very moment. Communism is but one instant in this long history; yet we see everything
through that red prism. We admit that there are differences
between the Russian and Chinese régimes, yet our desire for
symmetry makes us force everything into the strict framework
of ideology. Obsessed by dogmas, we tend to consider negligible
whatever escapes their limits. Now it seems that China eludes
Marxist categories as well as liberal ones, or else, if she sometimes conforms to the former, it is really through a return to her
own past. Images suggested by propaganda or sentimental
idealism are merely projections of fear or ignorance. The

spectre of the human robot, with which we are periodically threatened, is devoid of reality; the alarming, or incomprehensible, process of brain-washing is merely a particular aspect of the bitter crisis in which China is involved. It is a feature of revolution, and must be interpreted in the light of a collective emotion to which we might find parallels in every age and in all countries.

Dare we say that virtue has assumed power and reigns in China? Neither the old-time 'Chinaman' nor the 'robot' of the future will serve as emblems of a world in latent conflict with the rest of mankind, a China fully mobilized today, a civilization transformed and insurgent, because its 'humiliation . . . suddenly becomes a value, when it is no longer something to be escaped from but a source of salvation . . .'[1]

This is how China looks at the World.

[1] Malraux, *La Condition Humaine*. Gallinard, 1933.

3 - *Third letter*

My dear T'ang-lin,

I sometimes recall springtime in the well-tended gardens of the T'ai Miao[1] or visits to the summer palace or the Ming tombs in autumn. At that season the light makes the meanest stone glow, and imparts to the white marble of bridges and porticoes the lustre of leather or velvet. But I cling even more to the memory of those great Chinese winters, of our walks along streets parched by sandy winds: at the onset of the deep cold, all Peking overnight dressed in skins and furs—mink or rabbit, pelisses or tatters, an inspired rig-out. You wore your long robe of grey cotton, your black felt slippers, a thick muffler and your fur cap; fires were lit at street corners, and the dense steam of cooking food filled the icy evening air; while in the frozen midnights the long strident call of the tripe-vendor rang through the town. At such times I could imagine, I could observe, I could even experience life in medieval Europe, its towns, its fairs, its taverns . . . I rediscovered the forgotten antechambers of our past; I grew familiar with all the ingenuity and comfort of a civilization based on the vegetable kingdom, which was our own hardly more than a century ago. I grew indeed to love those winters; they taught me history.

From these images, and from so many others that make up my present picture of faraway China, tropical or frozen, I should like to exclude any exoticism. For a long while I tried to look at the dragons on Chinese pagodas with the same eyes as at those on the portals of Vézelay, gradually stripping those monsters of their strangeness until I could feel that they somehow belonged to me, and could understand them better. By an inverse process I sought to relate our Romanesque creatures to that East from which they are said to derive, so as to see them more clearly.

[1] A park close to the Forbidden City in Peking.

93

This two-way mental process trains us to judge unfamiliar things better, and teaches us some inkling of the incomprehensible, as though by some magic spell we were transported into the heart of each other's world—you hither, ourselves into your distant land—so as to be suddenly surrounded by the whole life of it, and not by the incomplete knowledge that brings only perplexity or an off-hand judgment. Space even more than time confuses the imagination. I am one man here, another man elsewhere; should I be writing to you in this way if I were at this moment breathing the air of China?

Seen from here, your country is like a strange coin, one side of which shows, in relief, the tarnished image of a majestic past, the other a gleaming ideological emblem. The Eastern dreamworld and the wholly political abstraction cannot be contemplated simultaneously. The blend of Orientalism and Communism is repellent to the rational mind, which discards the one impatiently and accepts the other with puerile sympathy or with contemptuous hatred.

I have known men who sang the praises of a bygone China, forever vanished. The disappearance of the pigtail or some other custom made them say, 'China is no longer China.' They had lived on the surface of things; they had delighted in the film of varnish which in course of time had flaked away. They had gone home disillusioned, leaving their lost paradise to whoever wanted it. I dare not speak like that, and I should like to tell the younger generation, who will know you better, that the old undying China still exists.

But are there not among you, too, some who, obsessed with details or seduced by fiction, base your concept of the European world on fragile superficialities? It is true that you have seen our soldiers, our merchants and our missionaries: the worst and the best. For a long time you were indifferent to their disturbing message. Then you felt its force. This aroused in your people an incessant and manifold curiosity, from which you yourself, as an individual, were not immune. You learnt to know us well, then; your statesmen and your intellectuals, came over here, shared our life; many of our books were translated. And thus by degrees the élite among you—men like yourself—communicated to the Chinese people their own vision of the outside world. But not to the point of loving it, not to the point of including Europe in your museums, your theatre. Your attitude was always a defensive one. You did not collect ornaments and works of art from our world. This difference speaks volumes about the nature of our relations in the realm of feeling and of mind. And the Opera, that focus of your consciousness, seems bent on perpetuating a state of mind in which Europe plays no part. The danger of carrying this too far cannot be more obvious. There is no finer fiction than the real experience of others. Your Opera and your novels might help you to grasp that reality more surely, and not to encourage China in that evasion which has become so perilous.

But to tell the truth, what Chinese traveller, absorbed in the effort and impetus of your Revolution, remembering your half-empty bowls and your rationed rice, your severe virtue, would dare to give an impartial and coherent picture of our abundance, our keen and sometimes unscrupulous activity, our restless liberty? Today I fear lest the tide of swelling passions should bring to your shores only the flotsam and jetsam of doctrines, from which you will derive only distorted images of ourselves. I fear lest Capitalism, Socialism, Rationalism and all the rest of the 'isms' may hide Europe from you.

Our paths, then, are diverging ever more widely. Our memories are not the best way of bringing them closer together. We must refresh ourselves with new images. Oh, if I could once more, whole-heartedly, delight in the thought of the T'ai Miao, of its trees, of its monumental gates on some bright summer morning when the flower-beds have been freshly watered and the early strollers breath the inimitable scent of gardens tended from time immemorial!

> *'The dizzy cliffs tear the sky apart*
> *The trees, intertwined, cut into the sun*
> *In the shadowy ravines the glory of springtime is dying;*
> *On the frozen peaks the summer's snows endure.'*[1]

[1] K'ong Shih-Kuei (A.D. 447–501)

In these days, when China wishes to make her voice heard everywhere and play the part to which she is entitled, each of us needs the truest vision of the other, and goodwill to understand each other. How far we are from this! In the great prospect that lies before us, surely we should take closer heed of each other's faintest heart-beats?

Chapter Four

TECHNIQUE

1 - Great walls

Economists rightly declare that productive activity involves nowadays so many diverse techniques and skills, so many tasks and functions, that it requires that special form of organization, the firm.

One immediately wonders whether those great monuments whose imposing remains have been bequeathed us by history—the Egyptian pyramids, the Parthenon, the Great Wall of China—did not require, just as much as the skyscrapers of New York, a 'complex mingling of technical skills in a mosaic of tasks and functions'.[1] This implies asking the following question: were there, in the days of the Pharaohs, of Pericles, of Ch'in Shih-huang-ti,[2] any forms of organization comparable to our modern business firms?

The economic development of poor countries, a key problem of our time, has proved unquestionably baffling to our finest efforts. No massive contribution of capital nor any army of skilled technicians can ensure victory over hunger and poverty. Something else is necessary. But shall we have exhausted the subject when we have spoken of education, training, organization . . . and firms? By no means. We must also speak of liberty. In this connection J. K. Galbraith raises a vital point. The firm, as instrument of production, he tells us, is a *synthetic or collective personality*, which can and must enjoy a greater or less degree of liberty or autonomy according to the level reached by the economy within which it functions. We must take a step further, and consider the autonomy or liberty of nations, of civilizations,

[1] J. K. Galbraith, *Economic development in perspective*. Harvard University Press, 1964.
[2] Brought unity to China in 221 B.C.

which are equally collective personalities, within which the firms themselves exist; and consider too, the more or less conscious, more or less free and voluntary participation of men in the functioning of the firm, according to the level reached by their particular society.

As we contemplate the Pyramids, the Parthenon, the Great Wall or New York, we may therefore ask ourselves what were the motivations which, from top to bottom of the community, made possible these vast and successful efforts?

The Pyramids were funeral monuments, of course, and one might readily suppose that high priests, mathematicians and statesmen held ruthless sway over a people of slave-labourers who were subject to total constraint. Things were not quite so simple. The administration of ancient Egypt was highly complex, and undoubtedly included a variety of what we nowadays call 'transmission-belts', the lack of which is so cruelly felt in certain underprivileged countries.

About the great achievements on the Acropolis we are already better informed. In spite of slavery and, no doubt, of the lash, the Parthenon celebrates the glory of the gods as well as that of the community which erected it. Here Demosthenes enlisted as a common soldier; here the worker was fully involved in his work. How could he have remained indifferent when Pheidias, 'general manager' of the project, or Sophocles, 'financial director', and often with them Pericles in person, Head of the State, went up to the building site to ensure, as we know, that the plan was carried out in its minutest detail? One would hesitate to answer, were it not that the monument displays a sort of technical and as it were organic perfection that speaks eloquently of the high degree of conscious participation among all those, great and small, involved in this mighty achievement.

As for the famous Great Wall of China, it is not the only one of its kind. On the borders of the ancient Chinese kingdoms everywhere have been discovered the remains of similar walls either abandoned or restored, bearing witness—like so many fossils or bones—to a sort of biological will. They were not castle walls, safeguarding some individual noble; they invariably

protected a city at least, and eventually a whole kingdom. At
first they were dykes of earth protecting the fields from flood;
then, raised still higher, they checked the invader. Hydrography
and politics determined their pattern, their length and their interconnections, until eventually the Emperor of Ch'in succeeded
in uniting them in an unbroken line of nearly two thousand
miles, thus defying the Hun as Pericles through the symbol of
the Parthenon had sought to defy the Persians, by means of a
political federation, by an Empire.

The Chinese walls are not monuments to a nation's glory or
prestige. Their twofold value, political and economic, and their
evident utility were such that the rich must have contributed, if
not indeed voluntarily yet with a sense of purpose, and the
whole people joined in a concerted effort despite the harsh
compulsion this involved. But there is another factor: to define
in this fashion the frontiers of the civilized world constitutes a
magical or religious action, implying beliefs held and rites
accomplished by workers, engineers and the King himself.
Ch'en Lin (d. A.D. 217) wrote:

> '*The State's great works follow the preordained plan;*
> *Come now, to work! and sing all in chorus!*
> *. . . . Long, long, the great endless wall*
> *Stretches out the length of its three thousand lis.*[1]
> *At the country's borders stand many sturdy lads!*
> *But in the homes there are many widows!*'

We do not know the names of the firms or companies and the
detailed organization of these ancient undertakings, planned
on so vast a scale. These three examples at least suggest questions
about the secret mainsprings of co-operation and co-ordination:
about what it is that stimulates individual and collective enterprise. It may be said that what is true for these grandiose monuments, with their spell-binding power, does not hold for the
small-scale labours of craftsmen and peasants, which are the
foundation of any economic system. But here too, it seems,
inspiration was needed. It can be observed that in most peasant

[1] Li: measure of length .. about 1890 feet.

societies, magic or religious ritual serves to systematize, control and order work, in the absence of 'modern' technology. Does this mean, then, that where the latter functions the individual is completely uncommitted and has merely to be a robot? This would be the risk if business enterprises and firms, and People's Communes, and nations and civilizations themselves, losing the necessary degree of autonomy and liberty, ended by engendering only indifference.

Contemporary China teaches us that the quest for 'national liberation' is the primary impulse of that effort towards self-identification, without which nothing can be accomplished. And when the Indonesian economist Soedjatmoko describes economic development as a cultural problem, he implies the vast scale of that problem.[1]

Puzzled by the incapacity of certain so-called 'young' nations to develop, some people would like to psychoanalyse the 'under-developed' peoples so as to free them from that ataraxis which weighs increasingly heavily on the modern world. The solution does not lie in that direction. Contemporary China is not a convict prison nor an ant-hill. The building of the Earth Dam, a work equal to thirty Egyptian pyramids, inspires today smiles and songs that elude mention in statistical tables, economic indexes or inter-industrial charts . . .

But does the American worker consciously contribute to the greatness of his firm and to that of his country? Yes indeed, for he bears within himself all the myths, all the rituals; he observes all the technical and social conventions that make up the efficiency, the stability and the greatness of his society. What would become of him if that order were disturbed by the incessant influx of alien techniques, affecting his innermost being?

The most imperative need is thus a psychological one. Men will accomplish nothing unless, step by step, starting at the level of the techniques themselves, they gradually rediscover—like the ancient Greeks, or the Chinese today—the boundless delight of living and toiling!

[1] Soedjatmoko, *Economic development as a cultural problem*. Cornell University Press, 1965.

2 - Invention

ANY technique from the simplest to the most elaborate is always the result of some deliberate, inventive, calculating and imaginative thought-process, which constructs the human setting, directs the act and affects the whole drama of existence. In our relations with nature—whether mineral, vegetable, animal or human—technique organizes life in its physical, economic, social and psychological aspects. Technique is thus in contact with and takes in the whole of life, it is a coherent ensemble of inventions, inherited, borrowed or improved. It modifies both matter and mind, for man is not only a workman: he governs himself. Every society possesses its own physical and moral technology, defining a way of life whose various aspects seem to form an ordered, balanced whole, based round some essential theme. All techniques are inter-connected—everyday behaviour with food, clothing, politics—from the most individual factor to the most collective. Every art has its own technique, every form of speech its own method, every belief its rites, every hope its secret path to the uncertain boundaries between instinct and education.

We commonly use the term technique in numerous connections, about intellectual or parliamentary activities or the 'seizure of power' just as much as about hunting or agriculture or mechanics. But it is only the latter sort of technique that we now consider really worthy of the name. One might think that 'homo faber', our peace-loving and industrious ancestor, had no other occupation than making adzes, and was unacquainted with anxiety or psychological conflicts. Can we really agree with Dewey, that pragmatical philosopher in whom the Chinese used to be specially interested, when he says that 'man only begins to think when he has to overcome material difficulties'? Of course not! And yet this is a familiar trend in 'European' thought.

Dialectical materialism, for instance, holds that the evolution of material techniques involves that of social forms: the windmill begot feudalism, the steam engine modern 'Europe'. This determinism is unsatisfactory, for if we cap it with the further theory that social forms beget mental structures, we reach the absurdity of explaining medieval scholasticism by the grindstone and contemporary philosophy by the machine! Whatever we may think on this issue, does it not express that dualism peculiar to the 'European' world, torn today more than ever before between mind and matter, indefinitely contrasted? We have on the one hand techniques for dealing with matter, and on the other techniques that deal with man; and between the two lies a singular discrepancy, characteristic of our time. The stress laid on certain material achievements, the improvement of our physical well-being, explain our constant use of this term technique, with which we are so infatuated that we think of it solely as a victory over hostile nature and an explanation of everything, and thus lose sight of all other techniques, or at least fail to apply to them the same inventive zest. It is true that the special character of our machines and of our physics, their achievements, the patent success and the almost magical consequences of the whole course of material progress contribute to our blindness. Our mistake is clearly expressed in that contradiction by which we consider 'technology' as something in its own right, a material recipe applicable in any country, and at the same time speak of 'technological civilization', a concept which is empty if it does not imply the spirit behind that civilization, and moreover a pleonasm, since there is no civilization without a technology.

Our physical technique is thus only the shadow cast by the sun. It is connected with science, claiming both to be derived from and to have begotten the latter; and it gives widespread currency, in incomplete and distorted form, to that rational exactness and that quest for the absolute which are at the heart of 'European' sensibility and thought. Science itself is moving forward in all directions, but to what end? It affects and disturbs all traditions of economic and social life, our own and everyone else's, it encroaches on philosophy and religion, and yet it brings to the technique of human existence, mental, moral, institutional, only that frail support of knowledge constantly improved, yet constantly in quest of self-awareness. A new humanity is glimpsed, and yet little change can be noticed in our minds, torn by a deep inner rift. Although we hold an almost absolute weapon we remain—as far as all human techniques and all relations between men are concerned—at the stage of intuition, of empirical invention, allowing outbreaks such as those which, from time immemorial and only yesterday, have set whole societies, mobilized by passion, at one another's throats. One French thinker, Mounier, has said, 'The constant increase of our material power has gone visibly beyond the resources, indeed the limits, of our social genius . . . Twentieth-century man is striving painfully to bring his soul and his body into step with his machines.

How have we come to this point? Why did 'Europe' suddenly launch out along the path of rational speculation and invention?

Francis Bacon is usually credited with the rehabilitation of the mechanical arts and Descartes with giving a fresh impulse to the quest for pure knowledge. This is the accepted origin of experimental science, which seeks to make us 'masters and owners of nature'. This special conception of the relations between man and the universe is older than Greek thought. But surely it required very special circumstances for the will to conquer nature to assume such importance: the accumulation of capital combined with the emancipation of the individual, for instance, giving him awareness that the power he had glimpsed was worth his passionate devotion? Or the weakening of faith, combined with the sudden widening of European horizons by the discovery of the New World? Pascal, at the same period, was warning us,

'Failing to perceive these infinites, men have rashly plunged into an examination of Nature as though they were in some proportion to her . . . a presumption as infinite as the object which they seek.'

And again, 'When I began to study man, I saw that the abstract sciences were not his proper concern, and that I was straying further from my condition by penetrating them than others by remaining ignorant of them.'

But the flight had been launched, and could not be halted. Descartes was careful to distinguish between faith and knowledge. Henceforward the two diverged; the latter rose, the former fell. Human techniques appeared to waver within a tradition the course of which the French and Russian Revolutions—the former political, the latter primarily social—did not alter as much as might be believed. Human nature has its rhythms, which it does not readily reveal; it will not let itself be hurried or forced, nor altered at whatever cost. Are the car-driver or the astronaut different from their horse-riding ancestor? Yes, surely, definitely different as far as their ideas of liberty, justice, political and social rights and duties are concerned. But not so different—worse, if anything—as regards feeling, love, friendship and hatred, or certain moral standards. That is why all our oldest techniques for living are still valid; they have come to us from so far back that they are, as it were, part of our own deepest nature. Could they change so fast? Caught between the roar of his engines and his dread of atomic destruction, must man be lost? Gandhi used to say, 'Modern life is not an incurable disease.' In any case, we are surely entitled to seek an answer, as did the philosophers of the Age of Enlightenment, from the past and present attitude of China.

Leibnitz expressed surprise at finding the Chinese inferior to us 'as regards those ideas that the mind abstracts from material things . . . . but far superior in practical philosophy. It is impossible to describe the wisdom with which the Chinese ordain everything concerned with public order and the relations between men, with the least possible constraint; it is incomparably better done than among other peoples.'

This observation might be interpreted, in the present context, as showing that human techniques at the time received closer and more searching attention in China than in our own countries, whereas material techniques were still at the humble level that was ours barely two centuries ago. The contrast between the many inventions of the Chinese—printing, gunpowder, the compass—and the little use they made of them is a traditional puzzle. Armed with these same inventions, we brought out newspapers, fired shells and sent navigators out on to the high seas. The Chinese remained, as it were, surprised at their own discoveries, suspicious of whatever threatened to disturb the natural order of things or alter the balance of the universe.

The gardener of Han-yin, in ancient China, refused to use a hydraulic machine on the grounds that '. . . where there are cunning inventions there are cunning actions, and where there are cunning actions there are cunning hearts. The man in whose bosom there beats a cunning heart soils the natural purity of his nature; the man who has soiled the natural purity of his nature has disturbed the peace of his soul . . . I am familiar with this invention but I should be ashamed to use it . . .'

This attitude seems very different from our own. Whereas we respect the creative genius of the Chinese we despise their empirical attitude, fit only for a pre-scientific era. We discard whatever is not rational and cannot be reduced to an equation. We forget China. Now the characteristic creation of the 'Middle Kingdom' is a form of technology far more concerned with internal mastery over its actions than with its effect on the world outside it.

The traditional inventiveness of the Chinese peasantry is still revealed in the patient and subtle efforts of China's agriculture today. We talk of her peasant masses, but we are apt to forget the farmer, on whose labours all her institutions are based, the wealth won from her soil untiringly distributed—like the silt of her rivers—in order to build elaborate social, economic, administrative and political structures which are techniques of psychical life, founded on the cosmology, the craftsmanship and moral code of the peasant. Régimes may change, but this permanent attitude of mind survives, together with most of its techniques, which explains that solidarity, that discipline, that enthusiasm that surprise us so much. Is there any country in the world that administers and governs so many millions of men? And could this have been achieved in a single day? There's no doubt about it: only a thousand-year-old tradition could have enabled the man in authority, faced with an unfamiliar situation, to improvise so effectively, and the citizen, in such circumstances, to co-operate so willingly for the common good. A practical and efficacious awareness was necessary.

As regards material techniques, one finds in China more than anywhere else a sort of complicity between the workman and the object he handles: whether he be weaving bamboo, carving stone or beating copper, the economy and efficiency of his action and the excellence of its result astonish one. To reach such a point more was needed, surely, than the mere accumulation of time, more even than a tradition of work whose effectiveness has been confirmed through long centuries. The shape of boats or roofs corresponds to mental attitudes and to a conception of the world. It represents the worker's dialogue with wood and water, but it also reflects the long, slow intermingling of instinctive, popular wisdom with learned thought. Any technique may in fact be compared with a machine which is propelled by electricity and which also generates electricity; born of a mental attitude, it propagates that attitude. The mentality of a people engenders its techniques, and through them begins to spread its influence. To use a current Marxist term, such is the 'alienating' power, experienced daily, of even the humblest techniques.

The Chinese formerly attributed to the 'Tao'—that impersonal concept which we shall discuss hereafter—the worker's skill and the success of man in his relations with the universe. If every technique is inseparable from its psychical context, we may thus suppose that the 'Tao' is still a living force in these relations and in the application of Chinese technical thinking. Of course

Taoism is not consciously recognized by contemporary China, but just as the most intuitive of 'Europeans' cannot refrain from certain 'rational' reflexes, or the most agnostic from certain 'Christian' ways of feeling, so the Chinese cannot escape from 'Tao' and other basic components of his mind.

Like the Chinese, we are adrift on a sea of techniques, where any extraneous innovation lingers on the surface for a brief while before being adapted, altered and absorbed into the depths. Material techniques: human techniques. Thus each world seeks to preserve its global and original character. Just as the Chinese have their junks, which reveal a perfect concord between man and the world outside him, between man's purposes and the means available to him, so too, they have their own forms of friendship, of love, of family life, of the State: techniques which have nothing to do with science, for they derive, like our own, from moral and religious attitudes which, in turn, they propagate.

In consequence of the gradual desuetude which has overcome human techniques throughout 'Europe', particularly since the decay of religious faith, men have sought to revive these with quick remedies. The various forms of collectivism (Saint-Simon, Owen, Fourier, Considérant . . . and Marx) aim at systematizing an economic and moral order, giving it a universal character in order to obliterate certain inequalities. Any system—these not least—involves a risk.

But China, faced with invasion by foreign techniques, runs even greater risks than we do. The glorification of labour and the mechanical arts involves an upheaval, a weakening of her 'psychical milieu', and all her human techniques are jeopardized while no valid substitute takes their place as yet, save that 'European' collectivism to which, for that very reason, China clings almost desperately, improving it, perfecting it, devoting to its service the infinite resources of her culture, elaborated by thousands of years of patient and empirical invention. Her Revolution is indeed a social and political one, but the State ethic which it has introduced bears too close a resemblance to her own tradition not to be profoundly imbued with it.

China is reconstructing and ruling herself. She is resolved to do without foreign experts, from whatever source. Not only does she refuse 'technical aid' but she actually provides it, in the deepest heart of Africa. We may smile at certain aspects of her industry, which are still those of the craftsman. What must not be forgotten is the discipline that makes them efficient, marking a triumph of collective effort unequalled in 'Europe'; and above all the existence of traditional institutions which have by no means been swept away, but may still be found intact, indeed rejuvenated and endowed with fresh vigour. This world has not been centralized suddenly, nor for the first time. It has merely recovered its central rhythms, which had for a time been weakened. This continental mass has not suddenly been cut up into new territorial units; its ancient provinces and their governments, its prefectures, sub-prefectures, cantons and villages are the gear-wheels in that immense machine which moves according to the traditional plan: the central law and the peripheral ethic coincide at the point where the élite—the Party and the numerous and responsible bureaucracy—ensure the essential transmission and execution of the general line.

The Chinese Communist Party employs methods which are unique and so special that one wonders whether they can still be considered as Leninist techniques, or have already evolved into something else. The long history of the Chinese Communist Party prior to its victory, its gradual seizure of power, may explain its effectiveness and its hold over the people. But is this enough? Is its basic concept 'from the masses to the masses'—that is to say, seek inspiration in the people in order to serve the people—a Marxist one, or is it the result of an old tradition of paternalistic philosophy? One may wonder, 'Does the Chinese Communist Party's concept of "the Master", with all that the term implies of intimacy, of devotion, but also of authoritarianism, derive from the Confucian tradition of the master/disciple relationship, a fundamental human relationship?'[1]. This sort of human technique cannot be improvised, and as we shall see, Chinese thought requires for its communication this didactic

[1] Enrica Collotti-Pischel, *La révolution ininterrompue*. Julliard, 1964.

method in which the Master is at once father, priest, leader and, as it were, the incarnation of the collective will.

Economic techniques have undergone profound alteration, although China is still a mainly agricultural and peasant society. The concentration of capital, a necessary condition of what is called 'development', cannot of course be achieved without taking into account the distributive network in which the Commune, comprising certain elements of the old order, forms an essential factor; while the rational activity of entrepreneurs has its place within an apparatus that is unknown in Russia. Thrift, that traditional Chinese virtue, is practised within a complexity of technical secrets and incentives, organized in an economic system not of consumption—which China has never known—but of widespread saving. Herein no doubt lies one of China's secrets, and her hope of a future development, which cannot therefore, for a long time to come, be fitted into any integrated system of world economy.

This development poses the same problems as that of any under-developed country, except that here we find an autonomous process: China wants to be, as far as possible, self-sufficient. This 'endogenous' process is not readily met with elsewhere. Its absence constitutes the greatest threat to those generous programmes through which wealthy countries seek to safeguard poorer countries as swiftly as possible against hunger, ignorance and disease, by trying to teach them all kinds of techniques which they struggle to acquire. Our experts too often dismiss what they call the underlying civilizations and techniques as being merely obstacles to the application and spread of 'European' techniques, whose ultimate aim is a universal economic system itself a prerequisite for a political organization of 'European' type, which would become world-wide by dint of imposing uniformity upon the world. But it is the same with political techniques as with any others. If the worker is not in harmony with his machine and if he does not respect it, industry breaks down, equipment and investment are dangerously eroded. If the citizen or business man lacks the sense of belonging to a collective unit which is a living structure, no measure of authority can make them take an active part in its development, and no genuine progress can take place. Institutions are nothing without the spirit that animates them. And that spirit cannot be taught from outside, for it is as incommunicable as an age-old heritage. Before this obstacle to the efficacy of foreign techniques, some people say that strong action should be taken on social factors, that we can alter men as though by some sort of surgical operation. But surely the reverse is true: if we first respect and then encourage each nation's spirit, 'endogenous' techniques will eventually appear. No imitation is possible, there is no ready-made prescription in these matters, and invention *from within* is needed in every case and always. The attempt to fit traditional worlds into the democratic uniform of European type—too narrow or too loose—is one of the more questionable phenomena of our time. In this respect China sets an example which all 'poor' nations are closely watching. Threatened by foreign techniques, she seeks to recreate them. She tells these nations, and perhaps all nations, that in our present day they must reinvent themselves, or else disappear.

The industrialization of China, which some twenty years ago had only a thousand industrial workers per million inhabitants, has now really begun, but is proving a difficult and painful experiment. However the political, intellectual and moral wealth at her disposal sanctions her optimism. Her tradition of human techniques, far from being an obstacle, provides her best hope. This is the case too, in some degree, with all other under-developed countries, even if they lack so rich and varied a past; but they will have to become aware of this before they can hope to gain from it. Hence the significance of China's example. These countries recognize it inwardly, so to speak, whereas we approach them from outside.

It is thus not enough to say that two out of every three men in the world are hungry, nor to try and feed them. We must realise what moral upheavals are involved, what resentment, humiliation and hatred. We must consider that the raising of the standard of living and 'development' are not only impossible at this cost, but that far from allaying these passionate feelings they intensify them, that the hostility of the 'have-nots' toward the 'haves' is aroused not so much by simple envy for another's material wealth as by the inadequacy of that other's approach. We have initiated industrial and economic revolutions, but we are too little aware of their effects, despite our vague anxiety. Our deserving but limited efforts are directed towards creating nations in the image of our own, piously hoping that they will preserve, willy-nilly, their spiritual heritage, if indeed we admit that they have any, if we don't dismiss them as 'new' or 'proletarian' countries, thus betraying our misunderstanding of the cultural factor in its global complexity, as applied to ourselves and to 'the Other', and to all the others. Some men sneer at the African statesman or physician, graduate of some great university, who seeks technical advice from the witch-doctor. Is their scorn really justified?

Far from obstructing a country's development, its culture—that's to say a certain form of sensibility—provides its only chance. This is the implicit message of China, whose influence may spread at the same rate as her achievements and her power, among all the 'under-developed' of the earth.

3 - Fourth letter

Dear T'ang-lin,

In your ports, where the sea-going junks are lined up in their hundreds, while shallops, fishing-smacks and rowing-boats score the sea in all directions, I once had a vision of maritime China. These fleets with their crews of sailors and fishermen, those high sterns recalling our historic galleons, the outline of the hulls, the tilt of the masts, the arrangement of the sails, all told of a highly perfected art of navigation and explained its contagious success. I have seen such vessels, which are said to have reached Arabia as early as the thirteenth century, throughout the Chinese world and even in mid-Pacific. Their shape has a changeless quality, as if they were a biological species which only some mutation could transform. These boats, typically Chinese shapes—among so many others—are, like your porcelain ware, a technical expression of living China. Your famous workmanship is not a thing of the past. These is a striking uniformity within each branch of the arts and crafts—as among the junks— over the whole extent of your country, and far beyond its frontiers: all the coppersmiths of China seem to have served the same apprenticeship, all your millstones to have been mass-produced in some gigantic factory . . . These objects, these crafts *are* Chinese civilization; or at least they are its mainstay, its manifestation, its visible foundation.

But there are so many invisible tokens, which are just as Chinese as the junks! Thus, the other day I discovered in my attic an old bronze incense-burner, brought back from China a long time ago. I bought some sticks of incense, lit them and stood them in the narrow upright vessel; then I noticed to my surprise that the length of bare wood of each small stick corresponded, to a millimetre, with the depth of the metal container. The only part that projected was that coated with sweet-smelling paste, which thus burned away completely. Was this by chance? Or did some very ancient system of measurement, a tradition maintained to this day, with all that this implies of invention and administration, of control and discipline, intermingle with those slender wreaths of blue smoke that brought so intense but fugitive an evocation of your world?

Your cookery and ours speak to us in the same language. All those simple or subtle dishes, inherited from long ago, common or uncommon examples of the art of living, of surviving, or of good living, are so many emissaries of the spirit that produced them. You use chopsticks, conscious of being ahead of us in this respect, since we still use knives to eat with. Things change very slowly where food is concerned. Events can sweep away history, but foodstuffs retain their form unaltered. Some long-dead civilization still influences a whole people clinging faithfully to traditional ways of eating as the last refuge of a vague hope. A whole way of life may be diffused by means of some mysteriously successful beverage: wine, beer, whisky or vodka, with the methods of preparing them, of drinking them and the social habits involved. Tea, which the world owes to China, brings into our homes at little cost, comfort and pleasure, meditative sipping, conversation, politeness and a touch of wisdom: the technique of tea-drinking the world over!

Thus, around any tangible invention there cluster invisible inventions. We are wholly steeped in our techniques. Just as China has her junks and her tea, she has her own forms of economy, politics, thought and hope. Anything she borrows she immediately adapts, so that the whole may retain, or recover, its original aspect.

But today, as you know, a violent storm is raging because certain techniques, not only mechanical ones, are spreading over the globe bringing an invisible train in their wake. It is rather like when the use of metal spread through a world where only stone was used. There's nothing so very new about it. Before the dawn of history men were already waging relentless wars because of the introduction of more efficient arms and tools. Shall we ever know through what rivalries, what vast battles, what epic struggles the invention of fire, bronze or iron eventually spread to all mankind? Within memory of man, however, certain significant facts hold as it were an after-taste of those unequal struggles. The plumed Aztecs, swarming for a brief moment round horsemen and cannon, then dropping like birds. Vast China yielding to a gunboat; Japan subdued by two bombs . . . Humanity is within reach of what tomorrow's archaeologists, if they have nothing left to examine but our material remains, may call the era of the machine, or the atomic age.

Being contemporary with these events, we are more favoured than archaeologists or historians or even economists. The earliest times show us whitened bones and yawning gulfs of darkness, but they do not tell what prolonged currents or sudden shocks, what sudden hopes accompanied the vast changes that we can observe. Political history is based on happenings the evidence of which is incomplete, so that we cannot fully trace their sufficient causes. Economics forces us to question its interpretations. We are privileged today not only to observe the universal diffusion of certain techniques, but to measure the effect of the invisible train that accompanies them, and even to be caught up in its turmoil. We see whole worlds founder there. We long, like Cortez, to save at least one of the conquered pyramids . . . but zealous monks, deaf to our pleas, plant crosses everywhere! Is the whole of life being levelled out, or is this just a phase in a great upheaval after which the whole diversity of mankind will reappear?

At Java, a few years ago, I saw in museums and junk-shops the whole paraphernalia of a dying culture—while the masses thronged to the cinema. As I pondered aloud over this cultural collapse, somebody said to me, 'Nothing has collapsed, things are evolving, that's all. There is less change in Java than in England.' To which I replied, 'In Siam, when a monk takes his vows, his friends and kindred carry him as far as the temple, lest he might crush some tiny insect. According to the Buddha, to take life, even unawares, is a sin. Now techniques take life, and we don't want to be aware of it! Things are being crushed, while we walk on uncaring. A form of life is fading out silently, without our noticing. History is being interrupted, cut off, stifled. A profound resentment is being born and becoming intensified.'

Does not the strength of these useful techniques lie in the spirit that accompanies them? Does not the force of that spirit, revolutionary for all its peaceable character, lie in the science that inspires it? And is not the devastating impact of that science, which all hold so pure, due to the drama it embodies— a human universe torn apart between earth and heaven?

A young man I saw lately made me think about these things. He had painted a girl's name on his car. Such, in our world, is man's relationship to the machine. Not only do we accept it with awe but we do it the honour of personifying it, as we do our ideas. We christen our boats Mary Jane; we write the name on the prow, where you Chinese paint only an eye! If the young man treats his car as a human being it is not through some embryonic rite of machine-worship, but a self-imposed respectfulness; a tentative dialogue with matter, when science has breathed life into it. He respects the machine as a prolongation of life, as the product of an effort towards which the whole of his world seems to be tending.

Is not this the 'invisible train'? You, in China, thought you could separate scientific technique from its train. As soon as she had borrowed guns, China became caught up in the whole network of arsenals, schools and democratic methods, believing at each stage that she could still preserve her essential values. You have touched the bottom of the abyss. You have felt the cold breath of nothingness. Hence your revulsive crisis.

The fact is blindingly self-evident, but is something *within* ourselves. You mistakenly judged us by our machines; we mistakenly imagined them to be universally beneficial, like the gentle rain from heaven, whereas they are sometimes deadly poisons and always formidable ferments, vehicles of what you confusedly call 'imperialism'.

The whole fleet of your invisible junks stands face to face with the fleet of our vessels in a titanic struggle. I see those great ships, your wisdom and your ethics, half unmasted, springing a leak, while their crews try to reach land on makeshift boats. You organize your defences, you block all approaches, you grasp science and try to conciliate it, seeing in it a liberating force for yourselves against cultural and moral servitude and a means of revenge, but also a necessary instrument for the construction of your modern world. Europe's industrial revolution and its consequences were, then, merely an evolution! Another Revolution, now, is beginning in your land. For science has at last awakened China and perhaps will seek there the thing we all hope for—that equilibrium which we cannot succeed in attaining.

In your poor but patient villages, where we were so often welcomed with the courtesy that you, T'ang-lin, know so well, with that sort of absolute dignity conferred by unremitting labour borne loftily, I learned to distinguish between poverty and destitution. Your country folk are rich with a basic popular inheritance, and they have preserved it well. Today our proverbial wisdom is dissipated along our motor-ways. But will your country places and your cities ever forget those 'concerted actions of Heaven and Earth', that cosmic spirituality and solidarity, on which is based your permanent conception of the world?

Chapter Five

THE INDIVIDUAL

1 - Protest by suicide

A Chinese peasant, during a lively discussion with other villagers, suddenly seizes a knife and thrusts it deep into the fleshy part of his leg. By this action he seeks to prove his sincerity, his truth, which his words fail to convey. Is he, on that account, to be believed?

Pascal said, 'I believe only those stories for which witnesses are willing to die.'[1]

Today, in certain places, we see men sacrificing themselves in the public square for such causes as the defence of their language or their religion. Do such causes justify such acts of unreason, such deaths? Must we heed the testimony of these suicides? Or should we regard them as acts of despair, born out of wretchedness? These individual protests are soon forgotten in this callous age. We say, 'These people do not value their lives as we do.'

To assess the importance of a suicide for a cause one must consider both the cause and the death. We admire Socrates for drinking hemlock and we know his story better than that of the Censor Wu K'o-tu, that great Chinese scholar who, in 1879, cut open his veins after addressing a memorial to the Throne which was classical in its nobility. There are cases where the human being thus transcends himself; there are certain paramount causes. There are also battles so unequal that to give one's life in them is virtual suicide. For this reason the value of a death is harder to assess than the value of a cause.

A monk soaks his clothes with petrol and destroys himself before a crowd of fervent and distraught onlookers. When and

[1] 'Je ne crois que les histoires dont les témoins se feraient égorger.' (*Pensées*)

121

where does this take place? It happens in Vietnam, at the fevered, tortured, unhappy junction of two worlds; a land long under Chinese influence, then under that of the Latin West, recently subjected to a distorted, jealous, militant form of Christianity and at the same time to a sweeping process of concentrated and hasty 'Westernization'. The age of the religious wars is over; the issue at stake now lies beyond their scope.

This human torch, a saintly and appalling act, cannot be explained on psycho-pathological grounds. It is a political protest, obviously, but is that all? This sacrifice, read in the context of the immemorial past of India and China, is intended to remind men that absolute abandonment of any attachment to the body, liberation from all personal feeling, the offer of oneself under the impulse of piety and worship, remain a supreme ideal. The Indian 'dānāparāmit-ā', the ultimate sacrifice, prepared for here by all the disciplines of yoga, that training of the mind to which Chinese Buddhism contributes both the authority of an historic tradition (holy monks throughout the centuries have sacrificed themselves in this way) and a purely Chinese inspiration, springing from earlier roots than Buddhism, infused and transformed by it. This is the spiritual reality of *Indo-China*, racked today by a deadly conflict between civilizations.

In the heart of Saigon, that deeply disturbed city, at a stone's throw from the cinemas where the flesh is glorified, this monk seeks not to convert the world but to warn mankind that certain pressures are unbearable, to prove that his cause and his truth are greater than words, greater than himself. How should one listen to the man who bears witness to so vast a crisis?

2 - Psyche

MODERN cities, glittering with a thousand lights and a thousand metals, mineral cliffs raised up by expert and industrious man, throbbing with complex and continuously perfected currents of life, incline some prophets to believe in man's imminent control over his fate. The exploration of the living cell, the breaking-of the genetic code, the fission of the atomic nucleus lead them to believe that nature has been almost conquered and that within a few years moral and religious concepts will follow the course of these discoveries, adapt themselves to the speeding-up of history and achieve some still unimagined mutation of consciousness, like that which probably followed the discovery of fire. One would like to agree with them. But the Chinese peasant bending over the soil absorbed in his age-old effort, and indeed all peasants (whom some are ready to declare expendable) tell us that we cannot go so fast. A powerful explosive, like a common knife, is primarily an instrument of destruction, not of life. What is the relation between suicide and life? The former seems simple compared to the latter. The infiniteness of things known and unknown forces us to renounce the arrogant mirage of mankind in control of its future, and to see mankind rather as ignorant, especially and primarily of its own nature! We should take careful note that the fate of men is governed largely by a past which is obscure and will always remain so, but whose reality we perceive within ourselves, at the very heart of our being.

The Greeks made us aware of our duty to know ourselves. Have we achieved this? The deeper we explore our consciousness the more we find it bound up with a complex whole, involved in a current whose direction eludes us. Each of us, however, while owing his body and his mind to the particular skies under which he was born, finds himself confronted with the universal as soon as he seeks to take stock of his being. An immediate relationship is established between the individual self and the whole of mankind. Each of us becomes conscious of man as a universal idea, and may feel an imperative duty to save mankind. At least, many pride themselves on doing this who nevertheless, through error, prejudice or folly, are in danger of destroying man. How many errors and crimes have been committed in the name of this fine ideal! To save man one must first look for him, instead of regarding him as an abstract concept. For man is not an idea; he exists.

'Western' man has a mental and spiritual make-up from which he can no more escape than from his body. Between the 'European' and the Chinese worlds there are profound and seemingly immutable differences which need to be explored. If the individual person is the essential expression of the human race as a whole, then the question is whether each of us contains within himself all the divergences that exist in man, or whether there is some wider reality above individuals.

The concept of the individual personality dominates many philosophies today. Adherents of various schools concur as to the existence of increasingly free and creative individual persons. They try to describe personality as a concept, but quickly recognize the impossibility of giving a satisfactory definition of it. It is so inward a reality that in order to grasp it, both as subject and as object, they are forced to have recourse to history. And they seek help from the history of Europe and from our Graeco-Latin civilization among others. They thus implicitly underline the correspondence between a particular form of personality and a particular society. And it seems that a civilized society constructs, over and above individual variations, an enduring 'basic mentality'. Great, complex civilizations like 'Europe' and China embody and bring to birth a sort of archetype, rich and enduring, with a strangely contagious quality.

Personalist philosophers say, not without reason, that in the formative years of our civilization Christianity suddenly produced a new revelation of the individual personality, and that this exerts a dominant influence on even the least religious of modern Europeans. This requires the parallel admission, which they are unwilling to make, that Buddhism, for instance, played a similar part in other regions. We should not forget that Buddhism, like Christianity, moulded many men for a long period of time. The Christian or 'European' type of personal life is not the only one; nor is the rest of mankind, merely because of its more persistent loyalty to family, clan or tribe, sunk, for that reason, in some profound unawareness. In point of fact we can observe in any stable human group of whatever dimension a character-type which reflects the fundamental importance at all levels of the enveloping group influences. The relations between the individual and the group, whether it be the family, the clan, the class, the nation, the civilization or even the whole of mankind, constitute in fact an equation whose data are variable, although the final result is always a human being. It is certainly not easy to distinguish the innate from the acquired, among all the manifestations of personality, the different characters, the expressions of sensibility, the ideas, beliefs and arts, all of which are more or less typical of the group at every social level. In this respect the character-type of the 'West' seems sufficiently different from that of China to justify the statement that the difference between them is no mere fluctuating variation which may easily be reconciled by some ideal, friendly arrangement. It is more a question of the character-types forming into different geometric shapes, like crystals of different structure, each one renewing itself generation after generation under the age-old weight and impetus of the community. To admit the universal nature of the Chinese character-type is simply to recognize that there can be two or more claims to universality. On this plane there is a basic conflict, visible in various forms in anecdote and in ideology as well as in the psychical material itself. One form of personal life is being threatened today. We must see how and why it defends itself.

True, we can accept, and indeed hope for, the upward trend of human evolution in things material and individual, but is the threshold of consciousness necessarily the same everywhere? Is there a unique and universal form of personality, the defence of which would everywhere adopt identical themes? Every culture, great or small, 'civilized' or not, has a word to say on this. Among so many original ventures, those civilizations whose authority is confirmed by their success, their long standing and their mass influence all tend towards greater individuality of type and a more richly-stocked personal world. In this respect one cannot but be struck by the flagrant contradiction in present-day China between yesterday's familiar picture of a nation of extreme individualists and the picture today of masses, suddenly become the most disciplined on earth. There has been a revolution, you may say. Yes, of course, but of what sort? The French Revolution of 1789, which arose to sweep away absolutism with cries of Liberty, Equality, Fraternity (a secularized Christian motto which does not appeal to the Chinese and against which they are in revolt today) made no profound alteration in our own character-type. At most one can say that it confirmed a tendency, speeding it up by a sudden political transformation, the effect of an internal impulsion. The Russian Revolution sought to free the individual still further and to this end began by fettering him. Seeking to deliver him from the bonds of family, clan or State, it brought about a certain social and personal disintegration. But institutions and régimes have to adapt themselves to the scale and form and personal reality of their citizens. Montesquieu spoke of a 'general spirit' from which the legislator must draw his inspiration. There can be no democracy with slavery, no tyranny among free men. But men are not exclusively bound or free. There are many variations, in which liberty and morality, having reached different stages, produce surprising patterns. Personal life is progressing the world over. It is at this level, far more than in battles or around conference tables or under the investigation of microscopes, that the future of humanity is taking shape. Herein lies the unknown alchemy, of which so far we can only watch the results. Here the essential process is taking place which will give rise to tomorrow's worlds,—worlds which will have to understand one another in order to survive.

The Chinese individual psyche is undergoing a revolution, or rather a revulsive crisis—we meet the term at every stage in our inquiry. A crucially important but much misunderstood process is taking place there, the clash of two cosmologies, a confrontation and at the same time a synthesis between East and West. The issue of this conflict, still uncertain, will bring neither side victory or defeat, but will certainly modify both. Let us attempt a comparison between them.

It is customary to trace the origins of the European personality solely to the Greeks and Romans, and there is no ambiguity about that. We know little, indeed, about what came before. But now, with the gradual and still uncertain dawning of a universal consciousness, lagging so far behind physical science, some modern thinkers are vaguely aware that history is no longer enough, and that each variety of the human personality has its origin, like language, in the darkness of bygone ages. The etymology of the word *persona* implies a mask. It was the custom among the Etruscans, we are told, to hang up in their homes the masks of their ancestors in order to give themselves a rank, a face and at the same time a clearer awareness of their individual existence. The Romans imitated them with busts. We follow suit with our ancestral portraits. These remote effigies are the tokens which Marcel Mauss had in mind when he summed up 'Europe' in this concise sentence, 'The masquerade gave birth to the mask, the character to a personality, the name to a unique individual, a being of metaphysical and moral value, an ethic and a faith, fundamentals of our thought and action; thus the course has run.'[1]

Our concept of the individual thus has the greatest possible measure of independence. Christianity, which confirmed the value of the individual soul and its eternal life, commands all our

[1] Journal of the Royal Anthropological Institute, vol. LXVIII, 1938.

spiritual attitudes. The 'European' personality seeks to be bound by nothing, often not even by God . . . Very early, probably at the time of the masks, a certain anthropomorphism asserts itself, which is still characteristic of us today, as our arts, our institutions and even our most abstract ideas bear witness. Thus we represent liberty as a monumental female figure of stone or bronze bearing a flaming torch. To those remote days we can also trace an anthropocentrism which makes man the centre of creation, maintains him there and haunts even the most recent attempts of our thinkers to reconcile reason and faith. Pascal said, 'What is man in nature? A cipher compared with the Infinite, an All compared with Nothing, a mean between zero and all.' Such an independent position would authorize our most daring ventures into the field of abstraction, where man, feeling himself liberated from almost everything, begins a dialogue beyond words with the Absolute, using the first person singular —prayer or incantation, pure idea, or deeply moving melody. 'Cogito, ergo sum'—or 'credo (ergo sum).'

The recent periods of our history display the excesses of this tendency. In art, in ethics, in politics, in philosophy, our romantics and our popular leaders, our artists and our entrepreneurs carry the cult of the rational and the personal to an extreme. Nietzsche explicitly denounces all intellectual or moral obstacles to the expansion of the individual ego; Gide rejects all social restraints. Things have gone so far, as a result of the surging tide of selfishness, as to produce by reaction a certain nostalgia for the crowd, for the mirage of social tranquillity under totalitarian servitude. The mind, agitated and bewildered, having reached the extreme brink of isolation and consciousness, is seized with fright. It turns then to ancient notions, tries to systematize them, seeking to reunite mankind around some reassuring ideal valid for all nations. Meanwhile, in the so-called free world, the break-up of loyalties and subordinations, which are nevertheless essential, threatens with anarchy a society where the physical emancipation of individuals intensifies a growing indiscipline, outbreaks of egotism, a weakening of religious or moral feeling, a slackening of all ties—marital, family or national. The least one can say of this striking trend is that it is disquieting, even if it heralds some new development.

Having thus briefly sketched the evolution of the individual in 'Europe', let us attempt to do the same for China.

In those distant days, while our ancestors hung up masks in their homes, on the other side of the world, in the valley of the Wei, the Chinese displayed ancestral tablets on their domestic altars; each was inscribed with a name, and set within the network of a complex order involving both the living and the dead. This contrast between the European mask and the Chinese tablet would be of purely archaeological interest, had it not been strengthened, enriched and multiplied, so to speak, during the course of ages up to our own time.

From the earliest times we know of, the individual in China has been firmly integrated into the group. The order of his birth determines a certain 'face', a strict position in the social context. The bondage of genealogy was early reinforced by a religious system which laid down and defined the individual's characteristics. Moreover the impersonal principle of the Tao, and later the teaching of Buddhism, assigned to man a place which was not in the centre of nature. It reduced the human personality to a mere episode in the cycle of reincarnation, at the end of which lay the hoped-for prospect of eternal oblivion; while endowing the individual, we must remember, with the priceless value of a microcosm, an autonomous reproduction of the universe itself. But Confucius, gathering together immemorial cultural elements, had already laid down a code of laws for the Chinese individual and had confronted him with his social responsibilities. This powerful moral teaching, for the past two thousand five hundred years, has kept the individual firmly imbricated in the collective structures. The following passage of the classic work known as 'the Great Study' might be called the Confucian sequence. It reflects the basic and enduring characteristic of China, suggesting that the individual there is thus profoundly and consciously involved in the social setting,

'The Ancients, wishing to illustrate virtue throughout the realm, first studied to govern the State well; wishing to govern the State well, they first set their own families in order; wishing to set their families in order, they first cultivated their own personalities; wishing to cultivate their personalities, they reformed their hearts; wishing to reform their hearts, they tried first to be sincere in their thoughts; wishing to be sincere in their thoughts, they tried first to extend the range of their knowledge to the utmost.'[1]

This sequence implies, in other words, that the individual is nothing without the State, the State nothing without the individual, and that the latter's true life, nevertheless, lies within. Family and State are, first of all, 'within oneself'.

And whereas Pascal merely says, 'One must know oneself; though it may not help to discover truth, it helps at least to rule one's life, and what can be better?'[1] Confucius declares: 'From the Son of Heaven to the mass of the people, every man must consider that to cultivate his personality is the root of *everything else*.'[2]

Which corresponds, in some sort, to saying—with a final plural—'*Cogito, credens, ergo sumus!*'

I think, and I believe, therefore *we* exist!

If the concept of the individual does indeed represent a basis for thought and action, these two attitudes are different, at least in relation to action. Here the 'everything else' of Confucius means China. For such is assuredly the basis of a moral attitude that is both individual and collective, of the profound sense of 'organic cohesion' of which China, both ancient and modern, confirms the reality and the effectiveness. This sort of institutional ethic, rooted both in the individual and the whole community, seems not to have the same force in our own society.

Today, just as the West is experiencing a sort of hypertrophy of individual feeling, so China is carrying to its furthest limits the involvement of the individual in society. She is impelled to this by two powerful motives. On the one hand the need to

[1] Pascal, *Pensées*, 81.75.   [2] Confucius, *The Great Study*, 4.

achieve what is called 'development': political revolution demands a strict conformity in behaviour. On the other hand, self-defence against a foreign form of personal life; the general mobilization of feelings is China's attempt to shut herself off completely on the psychological plane, to withdraw into herself, to raise a Great Wall of Chinese values against all assaults and infiltrations . . .

As we have seen, one may without exaggeration describe China's revolution as being, in fact, a revulsive crisis. For the clash between two mental worlds is not merely on a few intellectual issues, but on the entire content of existence, constantly called in question and subjected to almost intolerable pressure. This would in itself explain the haughty attitude of the Chinese, and our own, in our relations with one another, which is simply the sign of a daily intensified misunderstanding.

'European' influence in China thus introduces a ferment of transformation in all spheres, converging on the individual. Our own special heritage penetrates into a different but no less complex personal universe. Coexistence is forced upon ideas and feelings sometimes incompatible. Nothing is untouched: the self, the idea of nature, the relation to the other person, to the family, the group, the State. Love, ambition, respect, friendship, all are challenged at such intimate depths that anger becomes a protective reaction, pride a defence, hatred a strategy and contempt a reflex.

The family, the celebrated Chinese family, that foundation of the social order, but also, more than anywhere else, that essential nodus of the individual's world, is affected and shaken. In European society, individualism allows a growing indiscipline of morals and undermines the institution of the family, while at the same time Marxism claims to release man from family restraint and 'enslavement'. But the family means a man and a woman completed in a couple, and the couple completed by their child. And this social cell, the primary example of a group having its own density and inner glow, asserts itself as a reality, and like other social bonds explains the gradual rise of humanity. In the same way the nation, which also has its biological character, its educative force, its transcendence, as a necessary stage towards the universal, could not be suppressed or deprived of its independence, that is to say of that margin of collective liberty without which it cannot survive. A 'structural psychology' might shed some light on these problems.

The 'West' has thus sought to loosen to the utmost the bonds of family or nationhood, it has sought to suppress the emotional conflicts, individual or collective, the difficulties inherent in the family and the State. This mirage of freedom denies and forgets the 'fragile miracle woven by love, and educating love', denies and forgets the complex reality of the individual personality and its inner adventure.

China, where, as Leibnitz said, 'everything concerned with . . . the relations between men . . . is incomparably better done than among other nations', had been little by little attracted by our Western mirage. The 'hundred families' from which every Chinese claims descent were scarcely recognizable. Individual freedom, unleashed, was cruelly sapping the age-old order, already weak enough in itself. Reaction has come. And now the family, all the peasant or 'middle-class' families of China, cling to life. The new laws, structures and techniques do not oppose this; on the contrary. If we hear of a Chinese child denouncing its father, we exclaim: that means the end of the family, without thinking that for every such isolated case there are no doubt numberless examples of filial devotion. The Chinese Marriage Law of 1950 consolidates the couple; husband and wife share the property, control over possessions and responsibility for their children. This law goes even further: man and wife are bound to provide for the needs of each other's parents, to help them and not abandon them.[1] Does this clause also protect the larger family? This would seem to be the case, since it requires that adult brothers and sisters should maintain certain economic bonds amongst themselves. Our own laws are less demanding.[2] 'Europe' today builds houses, villages, institutions where a growing mass of old people of both sexes are undergoing the

[1] Marriage Law (1950), art. xiii.
[2] 'For this cause shall a man leave father and mother.' Matt. xix,5.

sterile experiment of isolated retirement. China seems still to want her old people; they are mentioned in the marriage contract. Traditionally held by the Chinese in almost religious veneration[1], they symbolized that ideal of continuous enrichment through the years up to death and beyond it, of wisdom in the personal and social spheres. 'Live to a great age, learn until a great age.' Is this motto still valid? It gave the feeling that one's personal destiny really reaches its highest point at the moment of death, and it powerfully encouraged that personal quest for model perfection, that transcending of oneself through social devotion.

Beyond the family there are villages, cantons, districts, prefectures, and those communes about which we have heard so much. These latter doubtless seek to regroup certain collective units under the impulsion of Party members, 80% of whom, it is said, are either related by blood to the men they control, or come from the same place. This explains the apparently spontaneous and voluntary character of the 'commune', which surprised the Russians themselves, obliging them to turn to Kropotkin for an explanation of so striking a phenomenon!

Whether we consider the family, the commune or the whole of China, we are conscious of an 'adhesive' force far greater than in Europe, the results of which, obvious though they are, do not explain its reflexes or its motivations. We have seen that one characteristic of any civilization is the establishment of codes and connections of all sorts ensuring tacit understanding between persons. We may well therefore seek to discover what, in the Chinese individual, are the forces that transcend his personality, what is the system of values through which this vital impulse or this social will is asserted. Some of these are evident, for they have a historic reality. Thus we may observe through the course of centuries the concept of harmony in China, as in 'Europe', that of freedom or that ancient and obscure notion of 'alienation' to which Marx tries to give a precise and rational meaning. But

[1] Confucius says, 'Nowadays filial piety means feeding one's parents. But we also feed our dogs and our horses. Wherein lies the difference, unless there is also a feeling of veneration?' (*Analects* 2.7)

there are no doubt many less obvious, less rational and yet quite as enduring reflexes which make up the popular mentality. We have seen that the Chinese Communist Party assumed towards the individual person the relation of Master to disciple. These are not empty words. Four characters are today inscribed on classroom walls, above the blackboard, in schools where more than a hundred million pupils absorb their message. 'Listen to the word of the Party!' This slogan would not have the power it undoubtedly has unless it awoke, in the depths as well as on the surface of each personal consciousness, an echo that could transcend it. Even more than the Confucian model that it suggests, this slogan identifies the individual with a social reality, and far from splitting or alienating his personality, provides him with a passionate enhancement of his own consciousness. The Party comes to polarize the collective consciousness towards a civilizing end. Thus we glimpse a fundamental difference between Chinese values and our own. Here, a rationalization of the individual carried to its most extreme consequences; there, a deliberate tempering of personal identity at different levels so as to safeguard a vital cohesion: freedom, by being more widely spread, is thinned out and thus restricted.

In the personal world of each Chinese, deep in every heart, live feelings which have been influenced not by the code of chivalry or courtly love nor by romanticism, but by a powerful solidarity steeped in moral and mystical faith, a cultural unity which, in so far as it had been lost, seeks to rediscover itself. This is no anthill, for all its myriad workers. The Chinese individual appears self-effacing, but he is not the dry grass in a waste land, rather the ear of corn in the harvest field! The Chinese have named no city, no street, as far as we know, to commemorate the ephemeral glory of an individual achievement, for the success they aim at must be complete, and therefore primarily an inner victory, conforming to that ideal which is no Imperial privilege but belongs also to the humblest man: the 'mandate of heaven'.

And yet we now begin to see in China certain modern statues of great men: the Emperor of Ch'in, who, two thousand years ago, mobilized China, side by side with pictures and statues of Mao Tse-tung. Thus, long ago, the Buddha's image appeared, where for centuries his footprint had been enough.

3 - *Fifth letter*

Dear T'ang-lin,

Let us explore further afield in search of our secret differences!
We have studied distant prospects, images, techniques both
visible and invisible, which have lifted a corner of the heavy
curtain. I am drawing near to the 'mysterious borders of the
Western world' and should like to linger there, for I can guess
that this is where our sphere of agreement lies.

I have indeed that 'long nose' which is your nickname for all
my fellow-Europeans, without distinction of ideology or
nationality. I also have certain less visible but equally permanent
features, which make me heir to all the characteristics acquired
by Europe through the ages. As the bee cannot escape from the
pattern of the honeycomb—which is somehow within it—I
cannot wilfully escape from that which shapes my life. It is less
precise than the bee's hexagon, yet none the less indestructible.
It defies calculation and manœuvre; it is the bedrock of our
minds and hearts. And I wonder whether there may not be some
permanent contrast between your bedrock and my own. This is
a difficult problem, for it is a matter not of knowledge but of
consciousness. Of course it is necessary to know and to understand, but also to believe. And I believe that you are closer to
nature. It is said that your society and the universe make up a
single 'system of civilization' and that the Chinese mind, more
closely bound up than our own with social categories, is less
attracted by the absolute.

Indeed, I see that science, the strictness which it implies and
the efficiency which it dispenses—for which we have developed
a kind of passion—appeal to you less than a certain sort of tradition, empirical successes, and the patient and practical quest for

happiness. On all sides I see proofs of this interpretation, which defines the Chinese. Any machine still appears to you as a stratagem, to which you prefer the recurrence of the seasons and harmony between men. You speak to matter more successfully, you try to win it over to your side, whereas we seek rather to dominate matter, to fight and conquer it in order to forget it. Perhaps we are cleverer, and you wiser? Our moral and religious contrasts might confirm this view.

Someone was saying to me yesterday, 'All that's done with. Modern man, everywhere, freed from the shackles of nature, emancipated from his bondage to time and space, can face the future confidently...' To which I replied that there would still be mountains and water, that the past could not be wiped out at one blow, and that it takes time to build a civilization. And yet, all around me, men are concerned only with building something new, with creating a fine, 'modern', human industry, facing exclusively towards the future! We are afraid of our former diversity; we believe that all the accumulated 'rubbish' of the ages will be dispersed like smoke in the wind.

And I tell you, T'ang-lin—for I believe it—that man is too rich and too untamed to be a party to such dreams. The ageless stream that bears us is not so easily diverted from its course. Only Hercules, or your great Yu[1], could succeed in such an undertaking!

We 'Westerners' often amuse ourselves by contrasting our slight but persistent differences: the Germans are musical, the Russians passionate, the English reserved, the Americans—those great 'Europeans'—we describe as practical, and the French as logical. You Chinese, too, make the same friendly comparisons between one another. The man from Chungking and the man from Canton make fun of each other's accent and customs; you delight in Chinese diversity, that precious possession.

But the men of two different worlds for the most part consider one another grimly, sometimes with mistrust or with repulsion or scorn. And this cannot be accounted for merely by political or economic differences; there's more to it than that.

[1] Legendary founder of the Hsia dynasty.

It is true that we Europeans, barely a century ago, were beginning to recognize our kinship, despite violent mutual antagonisms. Some writers are still striving to explain us to one another; their success is a foregone conclusion . . . Towards China, our attitude is one of great bewilderment. But that lack of understanding from which you, T'ang-lin, suffered when you were here must still be endured in patience. We could not then, we still cannot expect too much. There is about our differences something so permanent and so general that the only way I can find to grasp them is to try and imagine how personal existence is felt in your country and in ours.

In writing this I am not thinking so much of you yourself. In your travels far afield you have picked up enough to become a citizen of the world. I am thinking rather of some compatriot of yours who has never left China, a good citizen, a good father, a good Chinese, in whose ears the noise of the world still sounds so muffled that he thinks he can remain deaf to it. I have often said to myself on meeting such men, 'From the depths of that gaze forty centuries are watching me,' and 'What does his personality consist of?' For that's the real question. The personality sums up everything, but in its own surroundings. For the seaweed floating so proudly in its pool is but a limp thread when plucked out of it.

What is more elusive than that personal consciousness which is both illusion and sanctuary, a reality which cannot be isolated but whose force, coming from within, is irresistible? Living in your country, the most foreign of foreigners, the least accessible to Chinese values, cannot remain indifferent.

Such is the power of this contagion that it affects your conquerors themselves! The great Kublai Khan, when he settled in Peking in 1264, opened China to foreigners, welcomed the Polo brothers, the missionaries Carpin and Rubrouck and a whole train of 'Europeans'. Such concern and consideration were probably his way of reacting against the irresistible influence of China which was affecting his courtiers and himself. The Manchu sovereigns, too, thought to check it by forcing your people to wear the pigtail, a fragile barrier! The Empress failed to re-

sist. And did you not observe, as I did, how, during the occupation, the Japanese became Chinese?

When he first reached China our famous Professor Nasier lost
no time in donning Chinese dress. He bowed diligently, thinking
this was correct, and in conversation strove to make no gestures,
to keep his features unmoved and his gaze firm. He succeeded
so well that eventually he was captured and conquered by
China. His personality had become a hybrid. He had lost his
fine academic self-confidence, his imperturbable learning. This
process had started in front of the main counter of the pharmacy
in the Tung An Shih Chang.[1] The wall of meticulously labelled
drawers, the crowd of customers, the diligence of the chemists,
the self-control of their gestures, the swiftness of their diagnosis
all went to his head. This heritage, this empirical learning
accumulated during the course of ages, this copious and highly
effective pharmacopœia, made our scholar call in question all
his science and his own personality. He was an eminent man;
but a mediocrity would have done the same. Any foreigner, in
China, is like the professor in the pharmacy. Your Chinese life
is such a rich store of solutions and formulae that it is impossible
not to sample it, and be affected by it, and then call in question
all one is.

When you visit our countries the tables are turned. Your
master Wei confided to me that when he came to Paris it took
him six months to stop play-acting to his interlocutors and to
himself. For six months he gesticulated deliberately as he spoke,
at the end of which time he had become something of a
European. Back in China, he said, he went through the same
process in reverse, and the readaptation took about the same
time.

How are we to define this—which is far more than the mere
bewilderment of a traveller—if not by the discrepancy between
the inner realities of our two societies, of our two different
types of individual life? This we can best perceive by means of
the institutions, arts and thought and all the values which are so
many reflections through which the personality explains itself—

[1] The great covered market at Peking.

just as the wind is made visible through the leaves of the forest.
East wind, west wind . . .

During one of my journeys to Canton, T'ang-lin, you had
invited me to spend a few days in your big family home. I can
still picture the corridors and courtyards in which your brothers
and their families went to and fro and met one another, in well-
ordered harmony. In your late father's library, one almost felt
the weight of his presence still. Within the house there reigned
a calm which affected both things and people. You introduced
me briefly to your mother, your younger brother and his wife;
the others seemed not to see us, and went about their business
without being disturbed by my presence. You and I took our
meals together in a small room and this gave me the feeling that
we were alone and free, in spite of the conventions of which
I was aware all around us. It was then that I pondered over
liberty, which we defend more jealously than you do. As you
know, we once erected monuments 'to the glory of the citizens
who took up arms and fought for the defence of the public freedoms'. Have you, as a nation, ever thought—would you, as an
individual, think today—of waging such a battle? Would the
prior claims of hunger be enough to force you to accept unlimited restraint? Or is your personal liberty of a nature which
makes no demands, no violent self-assertions, which looks for
and finds a compromise on every level? You never knew Eleu-
theria, you raised no temples, no statues, no altars to that god-
dess Liberty. You never thrust your caps on the end of pikes.[1]
Perhaps this explains the difference. But Taoist liberty, symbolized by the fish, the slave of water, is none the less necessary and
attractive to you, provided the water is both clear and free!

So one must not thoughtlessly divide the world up into
countries old and new! We are as deeply immersed as yourselves in our traditions, bound to a past that is stronger than we
dare admit. The permanence of our differences can be measured
by the fact that they are not static. The adventure goes on without a halt.

[1] In Phrygia a cap thus carried meant liberation for a slave; the French
Revolution rallied round this symbol.

And today, you will ask, what point have we reached? My answer is that we are moving towards one another. And I am cautiously seeking, amid the glowing embers of a fire that still lights your world, for the universal meaning of personal values in China.

Chapter Six

MUSIC

1 - *Love songs*

THE Imperial schools of China based their teaching on a series of Classical books, the number of which, in the course of centuries, rose to thirteen. Attacked by pre-revolutionary modernists with all the more passion because of the almost religious prestige that surrounded them, these works, rather than expounding any strict doctrine or dogma, seemed to contain the actual secret of a civilization. China dwelt within them; and she still recognizes herself there. The Communists, following up the action of their predecessors, sought to divest the Classics of that sort of occult authority which seemed to hold China in a stagnancy that was contrary to the new spirit of the times. But they did not burn them or ban them.

Among these Classics, the *Shih Ching*, or 'Book of Verse', seems even to have acquired fresh prestige today; for this collection of 305 poems—love-songs and religious hymns—contains, as well as its purely poetic value, a practical moral message. Many of these poems, popular in origin, written in the old spoken language, have no doubt been recast and stylized in course of time, but they have lost none of their charm. In the first part, entitled 'Songs of the Kingdoms', the poems are grouped according to the region they come from. Tradition has it that the suzerain king ordered a collection to be made and translated of the songs improvised, in the various principalities of his realm, by young peasants, boys and girls, on certain fixed and seasonal themes. Later on, these old songs were sung at court, on special occasions; they took on fresh meanings and gradually came to be interpreted in a moral, political or historical sense. Henceforward the 'Songs of the Kingdoms' acquired

political and ritual importance, and the essential religious character that explains the survival of the poems and the use made of
them during the course of Chinese history. We can go still
further and say that the *Shih Ching* has given Chinese poetry not
only its gnomic power—its predilection for proverbs—but even
its characteristic symbolism and its style.

'In its sayings there dwells, together with that essential element
of necessity which is the prime virtue of any rite, the spirit of
spontaneity which is the motive power of all play. They possess
the complete effectiveness and the undying youthfulness of play
and of rite. They will never assume the aspect of outworn
metaphors which can take on a definite and abstract meaning.
They are live emblems, overflowing with affinities, bright with
evocative power and, so to speak, with symbolic omnivalence.
They go on unceasingly instructing men, with some initial
gesture, how to behave in order to help Nature, and they know
how to remind Nature herself, with a single sign, of all her
traditional duties.'[1]

Thus, for instance, these two quatrains:

'How well the peach-tree grows!
How many blossoms it bears!
The maiden is to be married:
Man and woman must wed.'

(Commentary: 'The peach-tree symbolizes the influence of the
Queen. Because she is not jealous, men and women respect the
rules; marriages are celebrated at the right time, and there are no
unmarried people in the country.')

'Now the plums are dropping
Only seven are left
Ask us, young men,
This is the consecrated time!'

(Commentary: 'The plums show that young men and girls wait
for the right seasons to wed. The domain of Chao Nan having

[1] Granet, *La pensée chinoise*. Albin Michel, 1950.

been subjected to the civilizing influence of King Wen, weddings took place in the right season.')[1]

We catch a glimpse, from this, of the special power that pertained, in China, to the poetic function. But what part does it play today, in a socialized and apparently extremely conformist country? To answer this we must observe poetic creation in contemporary China, in its humblest and in its highest reaches. First, in the countryside.

It happens that some peasant songs, still to be heard in the hills and mountains of China, Tibet, Tonking or Laos, closely resemble the age-old stanzas from the *Shih Ching*.

During the mid-autumn festival, peasants from villages tucked away in the folds of the mountains still come down into the valley. Young and old walk in long files down narrow paths. The girls, clad in dark blue cotton with white sashes, straw hats perched on their coiled hair, their necklaces jangling to the rhythm of their bare feet, swaying silently under their heavy loads of grain or vegetables, make their way to the great market. Towards evening, voices are raised in song. The assembled girls, sitting in the *shade*, fling out, each in turn, brief laughing snatches of melody on improvised words towards the group of boys, who, out in the mild evening *sunlight*,[2] send back answering quatrains over the heads of the crowd.

> A girl: '*You speak wittily*
> *You speak sensibly*
> *If you want to be my husband*
> *Come and let me look at you.*'

> A boy: '*Where do you come from, maiden?*
> *Where do you live, maiden?*
> *I'm thinking of you here,*
> *I had never seen you before.*'[3]

---

[1] Granet, *Fêtes et chansons anciennes de la Chine*. Leroux, 1929.
[2] Shade, according to Taoist symbolism, is female, sunlight is male. The singers' position obeys this law, and the song is thus enmeshed in the cosmos.
[3] Taken down in 1938 in the upper Tonking region.

These repartee songs are slight and shy, and might pass unnoticed did one not recognize in the eager messages passing from shadow to sunlight, from sunlight to shadow, the youthful and yet so ancient betrothal rites through which part of the Chinese genius was forged. For undoubtedly these peasants do not know the *Shih Ching*. Their songs, like those of the Kingdoms, are improvised in like circumstances some three thousand years later!

One cannot explain a custom by showing that similar customs existed long ago. We have to see how both are connected in enduring fashion to some reality. And the People's Republic of China is aware of this. Up in the hills such repartee songs are still sung, encouraged by the Party, adapted to the taste and teaching of today. At the festival, Miao girls sing something of this sort:

> *'Let's cut the millet!*
> *You speak to me, young man,*
> *But I haven't time to listen,*
> *For I must follow the tractor!'*

Thus a culture that is determined to be new adapts and revives its themes.

In the plains, too, and in the towns, another poetry, equally faithful to its past, shows that this art clings tenaciously to the people's life, and that this life intends to remain an art. In the Communes, it is said, there are public notice-boards on which anyone can display his own poems.

Finally, at the top level, the men who govern China also seek from the *Shih Ching*, and elsewhere, material for poems whose strict classicism, combined with obvious sincerity, awakens profound echoes in the hearts of the whole people, who learn them by heart and will doubtless go on learning them for a long time to come.

> *'The wind and the rain have brought back the vanished spring;*
> *The flying snow heralds returning spring.*
> *Already the thousand-footed icicles are hanging over the precipice;*
> *But the beauty of the blossoming branches is still there,*

This beauty does not claim Spring for its own;
It simply wants to tell of Spring's return.
When the flowers of the mountain blossom again,
In the heart of the thicket the plum-tree will be smiling.'[1]

Thus the songs of today answer those of the past. We might say, after Lao Tse: The dim past, 'Yin', 'motionless splendour'; the luminous present, 'Yang', 'ardent vigour'; from their union are born all the things of this world.[2]

[1] Mao Tse-tung, December 1962. M. Paul Demieville, who translated this poem into French, points out that it is based on one by Lu Yu of the Sung period (1125–1210). In both poems, he says, the image of the plum-tree whose blossoms, ravaged by winter, are the first to bloom again in the spring, symbolizes the poet's native land, which has been through a time of suffering . . . But whereas the ancient writer seems to revel in his despair, Mao Tse-tung exalts hope, and sees winter only as the forerunner of spring. . . . Among other allusions, in lines 5–8 China does not pride herself on any superiority, but she is conscious of knowing how to hope.

[2] See page 80.

2 - Beauty and goodness

CULTURE may be taken in its widest sense, as we have seen, to mean something that affects the whole of life. It touches on knowledge and on action, it culminates in science, in art, in moral teaching and in religion. Among primitive as well as among civilized peoples it is an expression of sensibility, a manifestation of mind within society. It is a *style*—literally, a way of writing life. Men are bound together by a countless variety of styles. These give colour to speech and ideas, to law and to prayer—like the sea, 'endlessly renewed'—to the fleeting strain of music and to the enduring stone. *Le style est l'homme même*, it has been said:[1] the essence of a man is reflected in his style; and this is true of all the varieties of mankind. From the individual to the group, from a class to a nation, to a whole society, there are all levels of invention and imitation, spread out and accumulated through time, preserving for ever some random flight, or echoing the imperceptible rhythm of patient toil. A quest organized little by little, then confirmed and recognized. The sum of numerous activities, each pursued for its own sake. Culture cannot be tamed. It wants life in all its richness, it demands and asserts its freedom, an impulse that nothing can control or direct . . .

And now culture has suddenly become a conscious aim in human affairs, a commodity to be traded in, a theme for rivalries and revolutions; 'new' cultures arise, nations accuse one another of cultural 'oppression'! This suggests that something important and serious is taking place in this sphere. Perhaps in the confusion of our time no culture is safe from the swarm, the surging tide, of styles?

[1] Buffon, *Discours sur le style*, 1753.

For many people culture means the fine arts. Well and good, provided the rest is not forgotten. Art organizes and educates man's sensibility towards harmony, up to those levels where feeling emerges into consciousness. No doubt this is why it offers scope for 'cultural action' of a sort. It is the peak that explains the mountain, and can be more easily contemplated. Art tells the story of a man and of his society, their crises and their moments of fulfilment. The masterpiece serves as a model, as a living spring in which inspiration is reborn.

Sculpture, for instance, reflects man's sensibility cultivated thus through the inventions and influences of successive periods. It tells of 'acculturation', as when Alexandrian statues followed the silk-trade routes—and of incompatibility, as when they halted, as though discomfited, at the frontiers of the Chinese world. This art stands at the highest level of inspiration, often religious in character: the tortured figure of the dying Christ corresponds and contrasts with the Buddha, freed from all suffering, supreme emblem of inner meditation. Angelic serenity or demoniac fury, everything has its place and its meaning.

In our European museums, the numberless crowd of human forms in bronze, stone or wood outlines or underlines the 'Western' conception of man. The quest for harmony of form—a longing for perfection handed down from age to age—reveals a deliberate self-isolation and detachment, a stubborn desire to give enduring shape to man—free, alone, the shining centre of creation—to contemplate this star from without! Idealised gods in human form, deified ideas in human form, the human personality made visible: they are at times the supreme achievements of self-intoxicated genius.

The Greek portrait allows us, over a gulf of twenty-four centuries, to ponder over the authentic face of Socrates. It makes possible an apprehension of his character so intense that sidereal space seems suddenly to vanish, time to stand still and the outside world to fade away.

The contemplation of the human body, made ideally harmonius, proceeds from the same impulse. From the tumult of his senses the artist distils and organizes his sensibility. Man, 'abandoned to himself', defines himself, reconstructs himself, to avoid anguish or despair. He moves outside nature, seeks detachment from everything; society dissolves. Art, we are told makes us what we are. Sculpture thus brings confirmation of that individualism, characteristic of the West, which was referred to in the previous chapter.

China follows another path. Her art is more restrained, more concerned with rhythm. Her austere and powerful style seeks closer kinship with the universe; the human form is held in abeyance. A Chinese vase—bulb or corolla—calls into play to a greater extent such factors as balance and mass and the pressure of liquid. Bronze or jade are subjected to a geometry akin to that of the earth and the stars. Natural objects—a cloud, fire, animals or plants—are concentrated into dense, perfected symbols, by some probing inner process of stylization which, while seeking inspiration from nature, refuses to copy it. There are no nudes and no portraits; man hardly features in Chinese sculpture.

Music reveals an important contrast between China and ourselves. Music is pure style; it is the true writing of life. Poets have warned us to beware of 'the man that hath not music in his soul', have called it 'the food of love', have demanded *de la musique encore et toujours*, more and still more music; and this art, which brings plasticity into the realm of sound, is taking an ever more important place in the civilization of 'Europe'. But indeed music exists everywhere. It has its strange and primitive forms; there are strident noises that serve to excite and rally and encourage despairing tribesmen. From its earliest and most elementary level, the rhythmic throb of a jungle tom-tom, music has developed, grown richer and branched out widely, without ever completely emancipating itself from the body, from the rhythm of its heartbeats, steps, gestures and dances. Music is all sensibility, the organization of sensibility, the cultural fact *par excellence*, defining and at the same time expressing individual and collective inspiration.

Through its subtle intermingling of melody and harmony,

it has become for us a spring and a secret of the spiritual life. Music becomes a prayer, a wordless upsoaring of the consciousness. St. Augustine described it as bringing about the 'Assumption of the listener and the Incarnation of the musician'.

If we still have the sculpture and the architecture of our Greek forebears, we have lost their music. We can indeed scarcely guess at what music was heard and played by the men who built our cathedrals. The brief but eventful history of our music shows how closely it is involved with the destiny of 'Europe'. Its various aspects and functions take shape according to popular themes: we have light and serious music, music for love and for mourning, for the family, for various occupations and groups and classes; we have chamber music, warlike music, ceremonial music, religious and philosophical music. Our Classicism assumed its definite shape at the period when Europe was experiencing a sort of plenitude. Architecture had come first, then in the course of five hundred years music caught up, and built those cathedrals of the soul whose style has become a pattern, unequalled and permanent. The rise of individualism in the nineteenth century found expression in peaks of romantic lyricism, while our armies, swept on by a collective impulse, were inspired to seek battle and death by warlike songs: national hymns accompanied the rise of modern nationhood. Thus our music shows us to be, like the Arcadians of old, pious in our sanctuaries, valorous in war and, sometimes . . . gentle in our ways.

Today our music asserts its essential value. The whole body of 'European' civilization, laying aside political or ideological divisions, enjoys communion through its classics. The same orchestra plays in London, Paris, New York or Moscow, traveling from one capital to another, and crowded halls respond enthusiastically. Radio brings music into the homes of a whole world of listeners. In the United States, the interest in music is not confined to an élite, but represents a general quest. And a single Russian pianist, having crossed his frontier, can do as much or more for peace, within one hour, as a whole clause in a treaty. While Europe was torn apart by war, the connective power of music made Duhamel say, 'Listen to the order of the

world!'[1] But this order seems as yet unable to rise above itself
or to renew itself. In spite of our musicology, searching passionately for truth and for tradition, music today is adrift among
systematic atonalities and vague borrowings, emblems of our
disorder, 'temptation of the West',[2] while in the United States,
for instance, there is gradually emerging a true symbiosis of
African sensibility with our own, of jazz with our classics,
reflecting a community torn by racial strife but already united
by music.

In China, music has no such ascendancy. It exists there, of
course, and has existed there for as far back as we can see. Religious music was taught along with the rites. True tunefulness
was associated with number; a theory of music was based on
arithmetical principles, connecting it to the proportions of
architecture and to the elements of the universe. Twelve resonant
tubes made up an instrument based on the relation between
Heaven and Earth. Throughout the Far East we meet an instrument called the 'Cheng', whose invention Chinese mythology
ascribed to Niu-Koua, who also invented marriage! Granet
points out that China's music probably began with this mingled
sexual and religious character, which the continuity of her
history helped to maintain, in a learned and religious context
and yet, at the same time, fulfilling the purpose that light music
plays for us. It remains at the level of an accompaniment or background to life—for funerals or stage performances. Thus today
what China chiefly requires of music is that it should accompany
her people's effort. Among the songs, the continuous flood of
music poured out in factories and in trains interspersed with
slogans, certain melodies can already be distinguished for which
the Shanghai Conservatory might perhaps try to find a meaning.
'European' music, like science, has taken root in China. But the
sort of fascination that sculpture and music have for us, indeed
the exorbitant role played by art at certain periods in our history,

[1] Duhamel, *Cécile among the Pasquiers*. Dent, 1940.
[2] André Malraux, *Tentation de l'Occident*. Grasset, 1926.

are unknown in China. Does this suggest a lack of artistic sensibility in the Chinese? By no means.

The Chinese genius expresses itself more readily in poetry, in the theatre and in painting. These arts are not distinct, as in our countries, nor are they the concern of specialists. Chinese poetry, listened to, is declamation; but it is also looked at, as writing, which is part of painting; it blends with and completes the landscape. That is why every Chinese is 'poet and embroiderer', painter or actor. These arts intermingle in Chinese life; they make up the general culture.

Chinese words, as we have seen, are less concerned than ours with expressing pure ideas. They leave more undefined. Their immediate significance is surrounded with an aura of suggestion, like certain musical notes that seem full of meaning, although this eludes rational interpretation. Chinese poetry, that magical art of which translators can give only an imperfect impression, may thus be said to play somewhat the same part that music does for us. The Chinese world finds contact and fulfilment in poetry as Europe does in its music. Inspired by its powerfully suggestive folklore and cast in an ancient classical mould, this poetry reaches the people through their opera, in which Chinese aesthetics seem to concentrate and art to find its right social function. It is this poetry and theatre that reflect China's true consciousness. In spellbound crowded halls, there flows from the stage a copious harvest supplying the whole community, from top to bottom and of all ages, with the emotions—historical, artistic, sentimental or moral—which are projected into real life by a dazzling make-believe.

Leaving poetry to consider painting, we may well ask ourselves whether the latter does not perhaps represent the highest achievement of Chinese art. Inseparably linked to religion, philosophy and history, Chinese painting, that powerful and highly refined expression of China's creative genius, is also wholly involved with China's life. From calligraphy, in which it is contained and compressed, it rises to the summits of a sublime expressionism; it reveals a stubborn will to grasp not man, primarily, but the very essence of the universe, through a study of its eternal forms. This painting is poles apart from our own. That subtle cloud may suggest Impressionism, but is something very different; and the artist who painted that reed bending before the storm, that almost tangible bird, was not copying reality, but concentrating on its essence. With the simplest of means, thus freeing him from the need for excessive concern with technique, the painter aims at conveying the maximum of expression. He identifies himself with nature, ponders over it, recreates it from within, but he never copies it, never sets up his easel by the wayside.

"European" painting, on the contrary, oscillates between an excess of illusion and an excess of abstraction. Today our painters are groping dizzily, their tradition having broken down under the double pressure of individualism and external influences. The concern with personal fame prevents the sincere pursuit of truth. Inspiration is widely dissipated. And some modern painting, the quivering, fragmentary reflection of too many things, seems like an emanation of our moral disorder, a despairing irony, frenzied with irritation and impotence, sometimes a financial or ideological gamble. It is the very image of our worried minds, of our technical inventiveness and our scientific excesses. Our professional artists are specialists let loose in a garden of cultures, who have lost their way there.

The Temple of Heaven and Notre-Dame, those anonymous masterpieces, teach us that great artists have known how to forget pride, to transcend their own selves and thus organize the sensibility of their age and of their world. Both tell us that these creations represent the exuberant harvest, the blossom, but are only one aspect of culture, which must include stems and roots as well.

Beauty in art or in nature may induce a state of ecstasy that may come close to the mysticism inspired by goodness. What is then needed is a sensibility coherent enough, highly organized enough, to bridge the gap between man and heaven. What will Chinese painting be like tomorrow, what will our music be, our poetry, or our stained glass?

During the present succession of grey days when liberty

seems to be dying, amid the fields and workshops of her vast country, China is becoming increasingly aware of an incalculable treasure which must be protected at all costs, even if this means sacrificing for several seasons, for as long as is needed, the 'hundred flowers' of impatient genius. And we in the 'West', while faith seems to be withering away in the great forward surge of knowledge, and the time that we have 'gained' is being consumed in inventions to further our material wealth and power, are also growing increasingly conscious of our destiny, a destiny determined by that past which we probe so intensively.

Both here and there, tossed about by these currents, a poet might well echo du Bellay's cry,

'Et les Muses de moy, comme estranges, s'enfugent.'[1]

Will not Muses one day return, here as well as there, with enhanced sincerity and a keener inspiration?

---

[1] (And the Muses flee from me, like strangers.) Du Bellay, *Les Regets*, XX.

3 - Sixth letter

Dear T'ang-lin,

In the Louvre, the other day, I was looking at the statue of Marsyas, who was hanged and flayed alive for having played his flute, thus challenging Apollo. The myth is significant, but so is that dangling body. From this image of bound and tortured strength I learn that five centuries before the 'scandal of the Cross' the tragedy of impermanence was felt and expressed in this fashion.

Our sculptures are eloquent, and you do not care for them. The nude does not interest you Chinese, and you scarcely ever represent it, save for those ivory figurines which your doctors used, in the old days, for questioning patients at a distance. When you came here, it was not out of prudery that you found this aspect of our art little to your taste. You were not shocked, but surprised, as you considered our buildings, where handsome nudities are exposed to the public gaze, and our periodicals, overrun with a far impurer erotic publicity. That's how it is. You do not put our statues in your museums. You are quieter by nature. The pursuit of a greater intensity of being, or of well-being, attracts you less than mere Being, or indeed a sort of Non-Being which we find rather hard to understand. On the other hand you liked our music. You often listened to classical records. You told me that you found in these something of that absolute which belongs to faith and science, a sort of harmony of heaven and earth that touched you profoundly. You understood the role of our music, asking me if its power did not consist in quenching a little of our thirst for harmony, concord and serenity.

We know nothing here about Chinese music; and I myself do not appreciate it, except when Wong plays his flute and through its rustic notes allows me to share something of his tranquillity. Here, your music is a curiosity, and raises a smile. Caterwauling, we call it, and enquire no further. And yet Confucius recommended music for the good order of society. But since his time the great Mo Tseu told you, 'Music is a shameful activity!' Was this why you relegated your rhythms, your tones, your songs to the background of your theatres?

The mention of theatres recalls to my mind a moment of the past. In a Peking street a poor man drawing a heavy cart paused to take breath. And instead of stretching out his limbs he laughingly assumed an actor's pose. Worn out with toil, he thus found in mime, in this brief flash of make-believe, a helpful and happy escape. The character of T'sao T'sao[1] had possessed him for a moment, as he haunts your foot-soldiers, your Ministers and Generals, and as all your civil servants recall the Han mandarin. What strength you draw from these centuries-old dramas, which the merest touch can make topical! In this theatre of yours there is so much force that I can well believe the story of the Chinese condemned to death who sang passages from some opera on his way to the scaffold. In our countries a condemned man may sing, but he sings something different.

For we live more intensely in our music; as Kierkegaard says,

'Listen to the way this life begins. Like lightning flashing through the dark clouds of the storm, it tears apart the gravest depths, swifter than a thunderbolt, more capricious and yet quite as precise. Hear how it rushes into our many-sided, varied life, how it breaks like a wave against its unshakable barriers, listen to the light throbbing sounds of the violin, hear the call of desire, the transports of delight, the triumphal intoxication of pleasure, hear that frenzied fugue, so wildly accelerated, ever faster, ever more untameable; hear the unbridled urgency of passion, hear the breath of love, hear the murmur of temptation,

---

[1] A famous general of the Han dynasty (A.D. 25–220) and a favourite character of the Classical theatre.

hear the silence of the instant, listen, listen, listen to Mozart's
'Don Giovanni'!'[1]

This power is felt, today, in our remotest villages. Music has
climbed to the peak of our culture and seeks to penetrate it
entirely.

> *'O listen! for the vale profound*
> *Is overflowing with the sound.'*[2]

I have often seen it written, or heard it said, that our civilization was in danger, was in a state of siege! Our borrowings from
the four corners of the earth have thrown us into confusion, our
frantic pursuit of invention makes us lose our traditions. Your
problem, in China, would be identical, if you had the choice.
But you are subject to an influence which is organized, one
might almost say embattled, and difficult or impossible to disregard. Our sculptors may draw their inspiration from Africa
or from Peru; with you, it's always 'Europe'. Do you know,
T'ang-lin, that last month, in sub-equatorial Africa, I went to a
concert of chamber music? while at that very moment the
Peking Opera was playing at a theatre near the Boulevard des
Italiens.[3] Thus the arts nowadays unite us with fragile bonds—
fragile, because they do not stand alone, and because there is
often a price to pay.

When you came here for a congress you expressed surprise
at hearing every delegate—the Frenchman in particular—
praising his national culture as though it were some cosmetic
product. You noticed that cultures are now something to be
bartered and bid for, as if the various societies were competing,
each putting the finishing touches to its achievement in anticipation of some Last Judgment. The fever is catching: we rescue the
Nubian statues, threatened by the dam—what's the good, if men
have stopped creating? If we save only the remains of beauty
and not life itself? The business man, the 'rational' speculator,

---

[1] Kierkegaard, *The Alternative.*

[2] Wordsworth, *The Solitary Reaper.*

[3] So named after the Italian theatre which appeared there in the 16th century
and had much influence.

hands over to the bulldozer the hearts of our historic cities if they are not thought handsome or picturesque enough to deserve to survive. Does the life of a neighbourhood count for nothing, from a cultural point of view? You Chinese know its value, having organized it so highly. Can art be so far detached from life in our countries? The architect is beginning to understand once again, but he is a voice crying in the wilderness, that geometrical wilderness which he himself perpetrated. If we could rediscover the centre of our cities, of our countrysides, of our very lives!

And you, T'ang-lin, have you found your centre? Have you destroyed, the better to rebuild?

Chapter Seven

THOUGHT

1 - The Educator-King

IN the second century B.C. there lived in China a teacher named Tung.[1] Twice a minister, he succeeded in imposing Confucianism as a State doctrine, which it continued to be until 1905. This alone would be sufficient claim to fame. But Tung was himself an original philosopher. His thought would seem to us today entirely out of date and somewhat trivial, were it not that, wholly concerned as it is with man and with human society, it helps us to recognize, as in the case of our own classics, the fundamental relevance of the intuitive wisdom of antiquity.

'We see,' he says, 'that man is distinct from the other creatures and forms a trinity with Heaven and Earth. That is why in the human body, the head is lifted, and is round like the vault of heaven. Man's hair springs up like the stars; his ears and eyes, with their keen sensations, are like the sun and moon. The breath of his nostrils and his mouth recalls the wind; his penetrating mind resembles the heavenly intelligence; his breast and his belly, now full and now empty, remind one of the infinite multiplicity of things. The multiplicity of things is closer to the earth; that is why the part of the body below the belt corresponds to the earth ... that which is above the neck is noble and majestic in spirit, displaying the characteristics of Heaven and of heavenly things; what lies below is full and humble, like the soil ...'

This may strike one as merely quaint, likewise the persistence with which Tung tries to shed light on human nature by observing the identical pronunciation of certain words. His conclusions nevertheless are important and deserve our attention. They can

[1] Tung Chung-shu (179–104 B.C.)

be summed up thus: man is by nature neither good nor bad. Education makes him what he is. And the duty of educating the people falls on the king, inspired by the sages.

Tung's authoritarian doctrine, based on an enlightened monarchy with an educative mission, made China what it is. The concept grew, overflowing the framework of political forms, until Confucius came to be considered 'a King without a Kingdom', and it has inspired the rulers of present-day China, for whom the education of the people is a task of paramount importance.

A modern French writer, recently elected to the Académie Française, setting foot for the first time on Asian soil, saw the numberless crowds of active, lively Chinese and asked, almost despairingly, 'But where is someone for me to talk to?'

It was pointed out to him that this was apparently an educated crowd, despite its exuberant vitality, poised and well-integrated. There were no clashes or insults, every man went about his business as unconstrainedly as possible. And he was told, 'Look for those who have educated this crowd, yesterday and today. There's the secret; that is what matters.' Because now, more than ever, great men in every country are Kings without Kingdoms, who by their thought and their example bring light to their nations.

Is it not time for our own kings, that's to say our writers, our poets, our philosophers, just as much as for those who govern our overcrowded, mass-dominated countries, to forget doctrines and passions and undertake a dialogue on the nature of man, on liberty, on everything, with the educators—one is tempted to say also the kings—of the most numerous people on earth, those educators whose writings, even more than their personality, point the way towards a limitless future?

That is why one would like to tell this Academician, 'Go to Peking, sir! Future generations will be grateful to you. They will think of you as an unforgettable forerunner, and—if you succeed in speaking about the things that matter—as an almost superhuman genius!'

Lacking such a dialogue, however, the world seems in danger,

prey to the confused anxiety that precedes cataclysms or rebirths
. . . There must be reciprocity in this sphere, and for this, in any
case, some preparation is essential.

2 - Contrasts

MEMORY seeks to conquer time. Armed with writing, it can leap across generations; enriched with literature, it can conquer space. Systems of thought grow up at all times and in all places, sometimes coherent and substantial, sometimes shrunk to insignificance. But intuition, ceaselessly reborn, clinging to the categories with which memory is stocked and to familiar processes, elaborates new concepts. The living and the dead, confronting one another in a vast, prolonged discussion, question one another's views on matter and mind, on action and knowledge, on science and faith, on being and becoming. 'Continuity and duration,' as Valéry said, 'are our most precious values.' We need both!

China's memory is long and rich; she has practised writing continuously for thousands of years; past and present are united in an uninterrupted stream fed by a copious literature.

Underneath the obvious differences between men there lies no doubt the common basis imposed by life. True, but each of us communicates with his forebears, subduing his spirit to their demands, guiding his conduct as though watched by those chosen judges whose example teaches him how to live. The quest is the same everywhere, but its results are infinitely varied With peoples who lack writing and whose memories are short, it is hesitant and clumsy; it acquires perfection when the storing-up of ideas becomes possible. The forest-dweller may have his own humanism, his knowledge and his beliefs, but these vanish in the atmosphere of cities. On the other hand, thought and faith which are rooted in scriptures, in a literary humanism and in a sense of history which provide their necessary, or superfluous, nourishment, can stand up to wind and weather. This awareness gives its colour and life to every concept, orders it and fits it for action. Thus systems grow up in which knowledge and morality, philosophy and religion constantly complete one another and intermingle. Man may be only a reed; but a reed with the power of belief.

Everywhere too we find an assumption of universality. The 'savage' pictures the rest of the world in the likeness of his own, peopled by men like himself. But his beliefs lose their strength outside the tribal world. His means are but feeble in relation to those marmoreal categories on which the world's cities are founded. These universal notions—one should say rather, tending towards the universal, since there are no universal truths save on cloud-capped peaks—are precious as patterns, which accounts for their spread, for the contagious influence of all rich, coherent systems of thought tested by long experience.

The scientific thought of Europe has this tendency towards the universal. It is immensely powerful, it has spread all over the world and seeks to assert its sovereignty over humanism, over humanitarianism, even over the very civilization that gave rise to it. In the same way the appeal of Buddhist thought in Asia is independent of family, city or race; from the very beginning it has been addressed to all mankind. Thus again Jesus bade his disciples go and teach all the peoples of the earth. There comes a time when all systems of thought thus aiming at universality must impinge on and confront one another, must adapt themselves to each other. History displays such sporadic encounters. And today an increasingly intimate and general contact can be observed between intellectual and religious systems, each in its full richness. Thus it is not merely men's knowledge, their techniques and categories of thought that must be adapted, but also their states of mind, their consciousness, their moral and religious beliefs, all concerned with man, but which in our time are attuned, so to speak, to different wave-lengths.

This immediately suggests a broader humanism in which everything would be fused, by which all men would be heirs to the whole world. But for instance, under pretext that the Chinese are living through a revolution, we deny that they are still heirs to Confucius. We are Manichean, since we seek syncretism; but we seek it only for ourselves, and in relation to ourselves. Now we cannot be heirs to Confucius. Our 'European' world will have no right to the Confucian heritage unless it give proof of some kinship with the Chinese sage. The Confucian categories, universal though they may be considered, only assume their full significance in the Chinese world. They *are* China; they have made her what she is. Confucianism, Buddhism, Taoism may be under a cloud today; many would like to think so; and yet Confucius, the Buddha, and the Tao are still alive to varying degrees of intensity in the minds of nearly a thousand million people, from Japan to Vietnam and elsewhere . . . Due to China's influence, they look forward to an incalculable future. We shall have to examine some day the way these four civilizing centres, China, India, Western Asia and 'Europe' —like the Four Horsemen of the Apocalypse—pursue their quest for the basic truths. We shall thus achieve not indeed any sort of fusion, but a certain common philosophical basis on which consciousness can be built up. We are far from that point! Yet the Vatican, for the first time in its long history, has now begun to search for this.

Some historians assert that Confucius and Aristotle both belong to dead civilizations. But with what justification? True, certain customs have disappeared, but has writing? Certain States have crumbled away, but have ideas? One might as well say, 'The shrub is dead, for it has become a tree.' Two great minds of antiquity have richly furnished man's memory, have bequeathed an enduring message and a way of feeling; there is nothing dead about that. Great men, Hegel said, are history on the march. They concentrate history in their grasp for a moment in order to give it a new direction. Thus Descartes makes us Cartesians, by gathering together what was ripening within us; thus Shakespeare, burnishing English metal, makes it glitter through the ages. Lao Tse and Confucius have done the same for China.

Of course we must distinguish between popular and learned thought; we must consider on the one hand the impalpable sediment, the source of all fertility, and on the other the 'hundred flowers' that conceal it from us. For underlying all doctrines, all thoughts, however well expressed and original, there is an 'institutional foundation', whose complex chemistry defies analysis, whose evident stability can only be perceived superficially, through its general structure or its coarsest molecules. We may indeed credit particular thinkers with the origin of certain great ideas; but these, luminous though they are, are but brief lightning flashes, due to the convergence at a given moment of factors as yet undetermined. While they last they dazzle and astonish us, so that we forget the human breeding-ground.

Ideas cling to words. We should therefore first attempt a semantic study, and then examine categories and processes, before tackling doctrines and systems. We ought to see how time and space, numbers and causes, for instance, are envisaged in different worlds, before trying to reconcile ways of thought which today confront and challenge one another.

Right from the start, in the sphere of language, we find certain irreducible contrasts between China and 'Europe'. Chinese words do not merely serve, as ours do, to note concepts: a Chinese word is not a simple sign, but a less definite complex of particular images, now verb and now substantive, endowed with the force of an emblem. Chinese is a language at once coarse and delicate, a powerful weapon for arousing passion and partisanship; it is a language of action. This is further confirmed by its script, a system of symbols revealing a concern with effectiveness quite unlike our own pursuit of intellectuality. It is ill suited to express abstract ideas, and yet has been extraordinarily successful as a means of civilization. It is the instrument of a way of thought which itself refuses to be instrumental, which is drawn less towards logic or the desire for knowledge and more towards action: towards wisdom rather than towards science; and which binds man closer to the universe, rather than cutting him off from it. This characteristic is even more marked when we come to study its categories.

Thus, time and space, those two systems of measurement without which man could not be assessed, have never been considered in China as abstractions, detached from particular events and places. The Chinese do not, as we do, conceive of some continuous flux in the course of which events occur, nor of some void into which places are inserted. Time, for the Chinese, is and always has been an aggregate of eras, seasons, periods; space, a complex of realms, climates, directions.

It may be said that by thus clinging to the concrete world these notions paralyse any true mental advance, and represent an outworn form of thought. But the relativity of our own 'European' conceptions of Time and Space, the divergences between our contemporary thinkers, the revolution which our ideas are undergoing in this connection should make us hesitate.

'Our' Time, which until recently was considered to be independent of things, has now in fact become closely interwoven with space so as to make up the fabric of the universe. This is Space-Time, which represents the phenomenal infinite. Within the framework defined by Einstein, Teilhard has conceived cosmic time, Bergson psychological time, other thinkers social time and social space. Whereas Pascal was afraid merely of infinite space, since the duration of the universe was, for the men of his day, limited to a few thousand years, we today are acquainted with the dread of infinite time. To this is now added the startling novelty of evolution, which is neither system nor doctrine nor hypothesis but a focus of consciousness around which cluster the scattered elements of our knowledge. In this vast movement, in this third infinity, evolutionary space-time, on which mankind seems to be borne along, 'European' Time has, by a devious mental journey, rejoined reality, and thus finds certain affinities with Chinese Time. This latter, whose relativity is expressed in terms of the duration of families, dynasties or cultures, is meanwhile striving to become coherent, if not logical or abstract, and at any rate universally valid. Our quantum mechanics have already justified certain manipulations of time, and Einstein's revolution, unfolding matter in time, allows one to imagine certain experiments—such as the space-ship travelling at top speed for two years and coming back to find our planet two thousand years older—which are in tune with the purest Taoist insights.

Such categories are not the whole story. The long use of them implies certain processes of thought. Time in China is conceived according to a cyclical rhythm. It is with the aid of a pair of symbols, the Yin and the Yang, that Chinese thought seeks to render the feeling of rhythm, the relation of spaces, times, numbers, dominated by the Tao, that sole motive power, that centre, entirely different from, and far broader than, our concept of cause.

The Tao is not a doctrinal, mythical or esoteric concept, but a notion which has become of prime importance, which inspires unanimous confidence in the Chinese mind, which is unaffected by the stormy flashes of contemporary history, by internal inventions and external influences. The 'Tao', literally meaning 'way', dates back to the remotest antiquity. As the 'way' of mankind, it is a moral code; as the 'way' of heaven, a religion. In either case, a profound and permanent source of spiritual life, inspiring among the Confucians a faith which, since men died for it, can be compared with Christianity, and among the Taoists themselves a mysticism which, if it gave rise to certain deviations and 'magical' excesses, nevertheless produced great models of the contemplative life.

For Confucius, who carefully shunned any sort of meta-physics, Tao meant the right way to human happiness. It was not a thing, but a moral principle to be adhered to unremittingly, if need be at the cost of one's life. It was also the Way to Heaven; but the Master refused to discuss this point, saying merely, 'Heaven understands me.' This doorway on to the absolute was further widened by the great Tao mystics Chuang Tse and Lao Tse to provide an interpretation of the universe, the forces of nature and the essence of things. Their thought is a mystical sense of unity with nature, no longer a moral code but, beyond good and evil, a quest for universal harmony, a passionate search into the depths of the unconscious. They draw from this the basic concept of 'non-action' which is not, as has so often been thought, a principle of inaction, but rather what might be called the Omega of Chinese spirituality. This non-action, with which the Indian Nirvana revealed its kinship in China, explains to some extent the success of Buddhism in that country. 'Wu Wei' (non-action), these two words were inscribed in monumental characters on the front of temples, in the smallest villages, in that land whose people have always been so industrious that it has been compared to a human ant-hill. What is this paradox? It means that 'non-action' is an injunction to *do nothing against nature*, to do only what is natural. Not to force nature! The value of this Taoist message, handed down through thousands of years, forbids us to suppose that the attempts made to adapt Chinese thought to a 'European' mould can wholly disregard it.

So, when certain of our scholars say that Chinese Communism is Taoist, there is some substance in their statement. They refer not to some religious hybrid but above all, and primarily, to the evidence of methods of thought and action. Their assertion is not based chiefly on Mao Tse-tung's achievement in swimming across the Yang-Tse river at the age of seventy, or practising 'non-action' in a famous retreat. There are certainly arguments to be drawn from this athletic performance of the President of the Central Committee as he skilfully tackled and made use of the current of the Great River—water, symbol of wisdom—in the pure tradition of the Immortals of the Taoist pantheon: a superb piece of political and philosophical propaganda. But it is even more in the cyclical action[1] inspiring the Chinese revolution, and its 'permanent' nature, that we recognize the influence of the Taoist conception of Time and its return. Revolutions, reforms and plans, all these 'leaps' describe a cycle in which numbers have an emblematic value: 'Hundred flowers', 'Five antis', 'Three banners'. . . . Whereas our reforms, the

---

[1] 'Practice, knowledge, then once more practice and knowledge, this pattern, in its cyclical repetition, is endless; moreover the content of these cycles of practice and knowledge rises each time to a higher level.' Mao Tse-tung, *On Practice*, 1937.

fruit of a way of thought that seems by contrast to proceed in a straight line, are always considered as being definitive and irreversible.

Chinese Time, then, is bound up with reality, with the concrete, with the civilized universe, with civilized space, centred not only on the individual but on all the enveloping groups to which he belongs and on the whole of civilized society; here we have a notion which has practical effectiveness, the secret, maybe, of that solidarity which we behold with such amazement. True, Chinese crowds may today be shown, in the Peking Museum, the wax effigy of their ancestor, prehistoric man. This sight may correct the idea of some bygone Golden Age, but is it enough to overthrow irretrievably that concept of Time, to make men believe that the universe had any valid existence before their sages instituted their civilization? In their learned thought and in their popular tradition, the Chinese are always conscious of owing everything to civilization: as Granet says, 'the poise, the health, the quality of their Being . . . They never think of setting above vulgar realities a world of purely spiritual essences, of attributing to man a soul distinct from the body. A single order presides over universal life: the order imposed on it by civilization.'[1] A powerful, practical moral system thus takes shape. This order requires a 'passion for orthodoxy' as well as wisdom; that's to say, a link between action and knowledge, between individualism and comradeship, all traditionally significant elements in the Chinese way of life.

And modern Chinese thought, at grips with that of 'Europe', seems to want to remain jealously faithful to its symbols, to its processes, to its categories, to the long-tested effectiveness of a system of social discipline.

If we seek to explain the special characteristics of our so-called rational, logical thought, we must first inquire into our means of expression, our language and our writing. Why is there this difference between European and Chinese words? We ought

[1] Granet, *La pensée chinoise*. Albin Michel, 1950.

no doubt to explore the biological origins of symbolism in our signs and gestures, the social origins of their rational meaning. This is a field that deserves closer study. If we go on to consider underlying principles, we tend to form theories, for example as to the origin of logical thought. 'The causality which our minds seek and find everywhere is an expression of the way human industry functions,' says Bergson, according to whom logical thought is derived from material technique, its categories merely reproducing the essential processes of man's action on nature. But what does he mean by nature? Is human nature also included? And why is this sort of logical thought unknown to the Chinese, who are such skilled technicians? One reason, as we have seen, is that we have been subjected to the influence of Greek thought and, since the Renaissance, to that of many philosophers and men of science. But this does not explain that peculiar characteristic of our minds, that dualism by which we set matter against mind, body against soul, existence against essence, the phenomenon against the noumenon. Science was born from this. The dissatisfaction we feel over the way it has developed is the symptom of that sort of disintegration that has overtaken 'European' minds, torn between two brilliant but divergent paths. Transposed to the social sphere, this would imply the division of 'Europe' between two 'cultures'—scientific and humanist—each increasingly incomprehensible to the other. And if we venture on the difficult task of reconciling science and faith, imagining thus the mental shape of some future world civilization, we are still dealing only with abstractions, with theories; we are trying to evade reality. 'European' thought, with its dizzy peaks, intensified by Christian dualism, does not provide a 'method of certainty' valid for all men.

Chinese monism, meanwhile, centring on the macrocosm or on the microcosm, does not pursue pure knowledge, either physical or metaphysical, but rather represents a complex of values in which knowledge and action, matter and mind, inseparable and continually harmonized, give rise to a consciousness which is markedly less anxious than our own. The existentialist revolt against thought, the spiritualist reaction against science, the many painful attempts to bring closer together the two poles of our minds would all be meaningless in China.

Today we must consider the psychological diversity revealed by manifold interchange between one continent and another, by a widening of our intellectual horizon, not as those eccentric philosophers did who sought to 'inoculate themselves with Chinese thought', but as an ever more urgent reality in the modern world. China shares in this movement. Her philosophy is seeking to assert itself once more, even while elements of Western thought penetrate it in a sort of continuous current. China has been affected by our dichotomy. She has rebelled against it, ready to fight with every means in her power to defend her own way of thought and present it to the world.

This way of thought has often been said to lack the religious and metaphysical element. But why should we assume the Chinese to be deficient in that burning impulse towards holiness which inspires men in all countries? Why should they not be acquainted with that faith which, when supported by knowledge, gives life and colour to the latter and raises it to the heights? No civilization can truly exist without that impulse, that supreme catalyst. True, mysticism does not take the same form in China as in Europe or in India. The vast trajectory of the Judeo-Christian tradition barely touched China; and she has closed her doors to the manifold springs of Indian religious feeling. But she has her own original store of beliefs, to which any extrinsic element must adapt itself. Buddhism entered China at the beginning of our era. As we have seen, the Buddhist Nirvana fitted readily into the Taoist cosmology; but it took six hundred years for the Indian meditative tradition to shed concepts that China could not absorb, and for Buddhism, transformed into something Chinese, to overrun and indelibly influence the whole of the Far East. Partly for this reason, Buddhism has been described as the Asiatic counterpart of Christianity. But it was not the sole creed to flourish in China. Side by side with Buddhism we find a Chinese version of Islam, so thoroughly adapted that today millions of Chinese Muslims take an active part serving the new society. The 'Quarrel over

Rites' confronted Christianity with the formidable obstacle of a self-contained philosophy, chiefly ethical, into which no other could penetrate without being altered. The fate of Christianity in China may be said to depend on such internal adjustments. It seems improbable that any religion should come to be considered there as 'the opium of the people', provided it preaches harmony and morality and practises peace and goodwill. As for the mystical sense, though it is, as it were, diffused throughout the community, its presence is none the less perceptible. There is a fundamental difference between Russian and Chinese Communism in their attitude to religion: the fervour displayed until recently by priests in the great Pagoda at Shanghai, the masses celebrated in the Cathedral of Pei T'ang in Peking, various Protestant sects, the activity of Chinese Mosques, implied a tolerance which was different from the anti-religious campaign in Russia at the start of her revolution.

If we attempt to look back over the intellectual panorama of China we are struck at once by its richness, its tireless inquiry, its frequent return to the fountainhead, its complex interconnections, its many schools: neo-Taoist, neo-Confucianist, Buddhist, Rationalist or Idealist, by the dazzling lightning-flashes of its men of genius: Confucius, Mencius, Lao Tse, Chuang-Tse, Mo-Tse, Chu Hsi, Wang Yang-ming, Wang Fu-shih, Sun Yat-sen and the moderns; we are struck, too, by the unity and coherence of three thousand years of continuous thought, displaying innumerable interpretations of reality and anticipations of the present day. In the second century, for instance, China underwent a period of great chaos. And the Taoist 'Yellow Turban' movement encouraged the suffering masses by preaching the advent of an age of prosperity and equality. Peasant communes were organized, food was shared and public confession of one's faults was the rule, all strangely reminiscent of the present day.

The point of all this is not easy to grasp immediately; but it may be affirmed that political philosophy undoubtedly remains the central preoccupation of popular and of learned Chinese thought. A pragmatical ethic was, and is, its predominant element. This is indeed a basic characteristic of Chinese thought, which has sought to unite mind and matter in a vast diversity of ways throughout every period in its history. The Tao Te Ching, a brief classic (81 stanzas), composed in about the 4th century B.C., deserves attentive reading, for its teaching certainly still inspires China today. Witness for instance the following lines,

> *'Man models himself on the Earth,*
> *Earth models itself on Heaven,*
> *Heaven models itself on the Tao,*
> *And the Tao models itself on Nature.'*

There springs from this a sense of unity with nature which, although it entitles man to strive against her at times, requires him to seek harmony and understanding with her.

The identification of action with knowledge is often implicit, and, moreover, many great authors have expounded it. Thus in the 16th century Wang Yang-ming comments as follows on a classic passage in Confucius: the disciple says,

'Some people, who know that they ought to respect their parents, nevertheless feel unable to do so. This proves the difference between knowledge and action.'

The master replies,

'The two things are divided by a selfish impulse. How can one know without acting? Those who think they know, and do not act, lack true knowledge ... Seeing a beautiful colour, smelling an unpleasant odour, are knowledge of a sort ... Liking the one, disliking the other, are action of a sort ... We see and we like; we smell and we dislike ... If my nose is stopped the smelly object does not offend me ... How can one know filial piety without practising it? How separate knowledge from action?'[1]

Chinese thought is inseparably bound up with ethics and above all with politics, in every school whatever their differences.

[1] Cf. 'If man closed his eyes, if he blocked his ears and cut himself off completely from the outside world in its objective existence, he could have no sort of knowledge ... If you want to know the taste of a pear, you must change the pear by eating it yourself.' Mao Tse-tung, *On practice*, 1937.

China has no arid dry-as-dust philosophers, out of touch with life, and unable to regulate their own existence. Every thinker wants to be like Socrates. Knowledge and virtue, inseparable,[1] are united in the individual; thought demands to be lived. Thus a moral attitude, valid at all levels, takes shape: an experience of living that would leave egotism and egocentrism far behind, and any interruption of which implies the untoward intrusion of the Self, the loss of the universe.

During the last century Chinese scholasticism disintegrated under the spur of foreign elements. We should need to analyse its slow development, the attitude of each intellectual struggling between two worlds while the mass of the people went their way undisturbed; and the gradual collapse of intellectual structures into uncertainty. We should study the slow working-out of contemporary Chinese thought and see how it makes use of all elements, even the most archaic, to mobilize the whole of China against the external danger of alteration and the internal threat of that 'loss of the universe'.

And while Mao Tse-tung readily quotes the best, and best adapted parts of Confucius, Lao Tse, Chu Hsi or Wang Yang-ming, while he attempts to interpret and apply the principles of Marxism and science, the foundation of his philosophy remains that unity of knowledge and action which synthesizes and gives continuity to the Chinese tradition. In 1368 the emperor T'ai-tsu, founder of the Ming dynasty, spoke thus to his notables at Nanking, 'I have come to suppress the causes of disorder among the people. They must all live in harmony with one another as they used to. Learned men who behave wisely will be treated well; those of the old régime who refuse to change will be suppressed.'

Chinese intellectuals of our day are compelled to go among the masses. There they undoubtedly discover the ancient idea of cohesion, of community, the feeling that the Tao expresses itself through the voice of the people, who have 'kept closer to

[1] As Dante sang, '. . . Fatti non foste a viver come bruti, me per seguir virtute i conoscenza.' (. . . You were not created to live as brutes, but to strive for virtue and knowledge.) Ulysses to his companions. *Divine Comedy*, 1302-21.

nature'. Closer to nature! The expression takes on a special meaning in China. A vast peasant community, almost untouched by outside influences, in which the individual retains his rich store of popular wisdom, arts and techniques: this peasantry, the custodian of China's dense culture, the repository of her spiritual heritage, is in control of the country's future.

'The strength of the peasantry,' Mao Tse-tung said as early as 1927, 'is like that of raging winds or torrential rain. Its violence increases rapidly, and no power on earth can check it; the peasantry will tear down any chains that bind it, it will rush forward on the road to freedom. It will trample underfoot all imperialist forces, militarisms, corrupt officials, village bigwigs and landlords. All revolutionary parties, all fellow-travellers will be subject to examination by it, and it will either accept them or reject them. Shall we be in the vanguard to lead this peasantry, or shall we lag behind, in opposition to it?'[1] During the course of China's long, eventful history the impulse towards revolution or resurgence has always sprung from the peasantry. Today a large number of intellectuals, having been profoundly marked by 'European' influence, are being forced to renew contact with the people, from whom that influence had separated them. By various means, by good will and persuasion, this élite is now being assimilated to the movement. It is making contact with the people; it must prove worthy of its role, or make room for a different élite. During the 'Hundred Flowers' campaign, the lid was briefly lifted to reveal some 300,000 'Rightists'.[2] These were for the most part intellectuals, and the highest percentage of critical attitudes was found among members of the 'Institute of Philosophical Research'. This evidence, among much else, suggests the size of this élite, its difficulties and the direction of its quest.

[1] Quoted by Mus, *Viet-Nam: sociologie d'une guerre*. Le Seuil, 1952.

[2] In 1956 a liberal experiment was launched with the slogan, 'Let the Hundred Flowers blossom, let the hundred schools vie with one another', with reference to the so-called 'Spring-Autumn' period of antiquity (722–482 B.C.) during which Confucius lived, among 'a hundred schools' of thought. But in the following year, 1957, a campaign to 'correct wrong tendencies' defined 'Rightism' as 'weeds to be torn out'.

What is happening today in 'Europe', on the philosophical and religious plane, whether consciously or unconsciously, among intellectuals and non-intellectuals, may well be compared with the experience of contemporary China. A sort of passion for history, an instinctive quest for social Time, goes hand in hand with a passion for music, outstrips ideology and sanctions a 'cultural' self-assessment in which the various nations seek to assert their identities, each according to its most basic characteristics, a differentiation which is at the same time a search for authentic affinities. This is an undeniable political fact. With respect to religion, the desire for œcumenism among Christian churches after four centuries of disagreement is evidence of a pressing wish for spiritual unity, while for the first time the Vatican seeks to make contact with other religions, accepted as such. A new interest taken in religious aesthetics seems to suggest, albeit timidly, a subtle but profound connection between beauty and goodness. There is, finally, in 'Europe' a desire for harmony with nature which finds expression just as much in a new interest in Franciscan poetry,[1] for example, as in the impulse that sends millions rushing off at the risk of their lives along thronged roads towards the untamed ocean or the mountains, to experience communication beyond words.

This brief glance at certain marked contrasts between the thought of 'Europe' and that of China may have conveyed soma idea of the intense and manifold effort undertaken by Chins today to recover her 'culture' at the philosophical and religioue level, both intellectual and popular. It would be a grave error to ignore or underestimate this effort. This revolution is merely a moment in time, an instant of reaction. How, then, can we consider as being merely 'oriental' and out-of-date, conceptions and attitudes whose basic message is that the whole man matters, and a collective moral code to be applied at the most practical and useful level?

---

[1] St. Francis of Assisi (1182–1226). His 'Hymn to the Sun', long forgotten, is a cosmic act of faith, great beauty and profound insight. Communion with nature takes on renewed meaning in the present context.

3 - Seventh letter

My dear T'ang-lin,

I wrote to you last time about music and the imponderable elements of style and inspiration. This time I must turn, not to more serious matters since art is a serious matter, but to a more considered analysis of our mental attitudes. I realise that here all our differences may disappear, that as in all periods we have had the same preoccupations, the same field of study lies before us. And I recognize parallels between Chinese and 'European' thought in their highest reaches, but at the same time different ways of thinking, processes which are not so much strange as difficult to transpose. Some ideas are almost alike and yet, because they have been built up differently, they remain so alien that it seems they can only be grasped by breaking into them.

Do you remember Hans? He had come from Heidelberg University with a degree in philosophy, to study in China. He had at first tried to compile a detailed comparison between your Schools and tendencies and those of Europe. He quickly gave this up. But he recognized the unrivalled power of wisdom over your countrymen. Professor Wei invited him to live for a while under his roof, and that was when Hans came to understand and become truly attached to Chinese philosophy. This seemed to you quite natural; you explained to me that Chinese thought is hard to demonstrate or systematize, that it requires examples, that it is a way of life. And doubtless Hans, thanks to the many aphorisms, allusions, fables and examples he must have heard and seen during his stay with that great thinker, must at last, like the disciple of some ancient Master, have grasped the essence of the matter.

Compared with yours, our intellect seems to act as an instrument, aiming at the high peaks of abstraction and too often forgetting life. Our systems, which at times leave reason exhausted, seem to you so many splendid evanescent bubbles of which, after a time, nothing remains but a faint trace of foam. The Chinese have been described[1] as 'ignorant of the art of demonstration'. Yet there are in your language plenty of terms like 'that is to say', 'that is why', 'thus', and other such aids to argument and proof. Obviously, conjunctions are not everything. There are the words themselves. And yours are very different, especially when written. Your characters, like highway signs, bear out your preference for action over speculation. They are respected emblems. There is doubtless something superstitious about the care with which your road-sweepers used to pick up any paper with writing on it, or about a certain country doctor's habit, when short of medicine, of making his patients swallow the prescription. Let us rather see therein the proof of the respect you bear to writing! Your literature reflects the broad outline of the thought implicit in it, oriented entirely towards culture and civilization.

Our intellectual methods as much as our languages seem to involve notable differences. I observed, for instance, that you are not, unlike myself, continually on the look-out for contrasts and antitheses, which are something basic to my understanding. You do not see matter on one side and mind on the other; you do not set subject against object, you see analogies and complete patterns where I grope on the edge of a mist. Instead of darting forward along brilliantly lighted but narrow paths, you graft the human factor firmly into the order of nature. And science, with its methods of reasoning, has no attraction for you so long as it remains purely intellectual, so long as it does not contribute to building up that unity of Being which is your experience and your life.

The broad lines of your thought have nothing in common with that mental alphabet which is constituted by our abstract categories—numbers, time, space, cause, genus, species. You have

[1] By Leibnitz.

the pair Yin and Yang, the Tao, and many other signs around which your world revolves, giving you an efficacious awareness, the secret of a harmony which you pursue unremittingly.

When Renan declared that science was to be the true religion of the future, some of his opponents described science as bankrupt. We no longer speak in such terms; but we are inclined to think with Pascal that 'the knowledge of external things will not comfort me, in time of affliction, for my ignorance of moral things; but the knowledge of moral behaviour will always comfort me for my ignorance of external science.' Certain existentialists are intuitively searching for what you Chinese have already found, in their reaction against an excess of philosophy of ideas,[1] against any system of absolutes, against the systematizing of systems, of which Hegel provides an extreme example. But surely this existentialism, which interests China—since it is studied today at the University of Peking—is still very remote from yourselves, since it is wholly preoccupied with the individual and his existence?

This calls to mind Teilhard whom we both knew in China, and whom I can still picture striding through the narrow streets and suburbs and outskirts of Peking, with bowed head and a subtle smile on his lips, holding forth about Man, the Earth, the Atom. You listened, as I did, to his version of evolution—'sacred' evolution. After years in China he still could not speak your language. From his attitude I had the impression that his mind, intensely fixed on past and future ages, considered Chinese civilization as a mammoth struggling against an ineluctable law of natural selection, as an ontological experiment faced with insuperable forces.

But in point of fact, on his first coming to China many years earlier, he had experienced an 'existential shock' comparable to that felt by the learned Nasier in the pharmacy of Tung An Shih Chang. Teilhard perceived China's psychical reality as well as her mass, and the profound differences that divide us. He thought that they could not be got rid of without an effort at mental and social adaptation on your part. And yet he felt that China could

[1] Against 'Ideosophy', as Jacques Maritain calls it.

not take part in the process of human evolution without profoundly modifying it, particularly in the sphere of religion. Thus he guessed at the significance of China's message rather than actually knowing it. And I sometimes wonder whether his thought, like that of the existentialists, does not coincide with your own in some respects. We can trace some echo of the Tao in his cosmic system, which binds man closely to matter, and in the basic ethic he derives therefrom. But Teilhard, as a European and as a Christian, immediately parts company from you when he puts man at the summit of creation, when he looks at space and time with the eyes of a scientist, when he attempts the hard task of reconciling science and faith, constructs a system of philosophy, and loses sight of the cultural diversity of man's spirit.

And yet he had asked himself many questions about those ideas that spread spontaneously and those that seem fenced in by walls, saying to me, 'When one has to pay for a religion to spread, there's something wrong.' This brings me to consider Buddhism, which spread as if naturally throughout China where it left its mark and was in turn affected: its influence coinciding with China's. How is one to accept the current notion that you are not a religious people? I have seen many proofs of the fervour with which you practise Buddhism. Do you remember the journey we made together to the summit of mount Heng? At the monastery where we stayed, we were woken before dawn, at our own request, to attend morning service. Hidden behind a pillar in the temple, we watched an unforgettable sight: in the flickering candlelight, to the sound of the wooden drum, we saw the monks transfigured by religious ecstasy. And so Buddhism reminds me of our many problems.

One of the great figures of the People's Republic, on arriving in Geneva for a conference some years ago, visited the statue of Jean-Jacques Rousseau and stood before it, rapt in thought. Then he straightway composed a poem . . . People found this incident strange and funny. But for my part I see in it a significant gesture; quietly, with deliberate tact, it underlines the drama of our time.

There are obviously in Rousseau, whose statue is still respected in Saigon, several characteristics likely to attract the Chinese mind. Like France's other 'Philosophes' he tried to understand China. In him and in yourselves today I recognize the same intensity, the same dislike of moral confusion, the same quest for new truths, the same spirit of innovation. His thought caused an upheaval in our world, but its message is not yet exhausted. This solitary roamer thought deeply about the harmony of nature; he would not consent to man's systematic struggle against it. That is where your Chinese thought, diverging from that of the materialists, coincides with his. Then again, this individualist insists on a Social Contract,

'Each of us', he says, 'hands over his self to the community, and submits all his power to the supreme guidance of the general will.'

He examines the nature of this 'general will', that inward light that is passed on from one citizen to another and which today makes each of you Chinese hand over your self, with all its power, to the community.

One may well wish that some day a 'European' statesman, visiting Peking, might go to the Temple of Heaven, not as a curious sightseer but in order to meditate, as with good reason he might, on what it is that made, and still makes, China great!

Chapter Eight

PASSIONS

1 - *Cultural oppression*

THE more we yearn to delay the outbreak of physical violence, the more culture becomes the key to international relations. This is because it provides considerable scope for violence of speech. During the past ten years, for instance, the phrase 'cultural oppression' has become part of the international vocabulary.[1] Nations emancipated from colonial status, all in varying degrees, display a certain cultural nationalism, while the old concepts of imperialism and aggression take on a new meaning. In this new situation, the whole world is groping and experimenting. Some words have a violent impact due to the intensity of the feelings they express; in such a case, they are frenzied. This 'cultural oppression', denounced in Canada as well as in China, seems to herald an acute general crisis. It inspires insults, provocation, all the language that stirs up rival camps to courage or madness, forerunners of war's deadly confrontations. Each side, confusedly mingling under this heading technique and language, education, science, religion and civilization, seeks to defend a way of life, a set of beliefs, to preserve an identity, to promote, in certain cases, a 'national' culture in opposition to the 'corrupt culture of imperialism'. Each, in short, seeks to safeguard its spirit.

But the ways of the spirit are past finding out. They baffle even the god of war. Victorious Rome was hellenized: *Graecia capta ferum victorem cepit*.[2] War, it has been said, is another form of politics; but it is also the pursuit, by violent means, of everything else. The clash of mentalities in battle is yet another form of cultural exchange, at the deepest level.

[1] First Afro-Asian Conference at Bandung (1955).
[2] Horace, Ep. II, 1.156.

191

In its physical sense, oppression means difficulty in breathing. Perhaps we should borrow this image to understand the internal dynamism of societies clamouring fiercely for a 'liberation' that comes under none of the usual categories. And if we speak of cultural 'aggression' we should also see this in its immediate sense as an unprovoked attack, an encroachment on another's realm, no matter on what pretext. It calls for self-defence, for protection, for a counter-stroke not only against violence but against that which corrodes and blights.

China, for her part, has had long experience of that cultural oppression we hear so much about nowadays. Although never colonized in the familiar sense of the word, China was, during the modern era, invaded on all sides by a confused, convergent flood of elusive 'imperialisms', great and small, which fused into a spearhead (of largely Anglo-Saxon alloy) so tempered as to resist her contact even while penetrating her. This influence did not, as in the case of a colony, take place within determined limits, with the restrictions but also with the reciprocity inherent in a two-sided political system. China thus became acquainted with that protean 'West' which so many other nations, less well armed than she is, are also striving to resist. The oppression and aggression which were so strongly resented consisted not so much in 'unfair treaties', in cheap cotton and opium poured into her ports, not so much in the techniques, the capital, the ideas purveyed by the well-meaning crowd of experts and missionaries of all nations; it was, rather, a feeling that the benefits conferred by the 'West' were likely to cost her the better part of herself. It was also a confused awareness that this elusive, irresponsible, technically efficient 'West' was itself losing, in contact with China, its own identity, prefiguring a false synthesis, a reduction of mankind to uniformity and excluding the diversity which must be safeguarded for the world.

'Friendship between nations, like that between two human beings, requires the fulfilment of each personality in its fullest individuality, rather than their absorption into similarity.'[1]
That is why the indignation of purists at the insidious pene-

[1] René Habachi, Chroniques, *Esprit*, April 1965.

tration of some foreign word into their language, though doubt-less justified, shows an excessive jealousy, considering that in other regions not language alone, but the whole of life is affected by large-scale intrusions so sudden as to constitute oppression. Must the remedy be 'laissez-faire' or free trade, or shall we at last witness the emergence of a moral code, of laws and pacts which will safeguard that irreplaceable diversity without which a world civilization would be a mere masquerade?

Freedom to be oneself has become, and will remain, a burning issue in the political world today!

2 - A Third World?

THE idea of a 'third world' is gaining ground. These two words are familiar enough today, and a hidden force seems bent on freeing them from the inverted commas which, through some lingering scruple, some still attach to them. They imply a world divided into two camps, from each of which, amid the tensions of a cold war, men scan with anxious impatience that no man's land which must be won in order to tip the balance in their favour. Some feel about this Third World that, like the Third Estate on the even of the French Revolution, 'it is nothing yet, but it will be everything'. Yet how can the other nations be grouped together as Nobility or Clergy?

To avoid such partitioning, with its warlike implications, we instinctively turn to economics. The very idea of under-developed countries divides the world into rich nations on the one hand and poor nations on the other. Two camps again, but which do not correspond to the first. There are no precise frontiers between poverty and wealth, and moreover it is hard to see where a 'third world' could be situated on the purely economic plane. So against our will, against our better judgment, we revert to the earlier notion, after subtly working out a complex evaluation of alliances, régimes and standards of living.

Economic development, it so happens, does not depend on adherence to one or the other camp. The preceding pages have sought to demonstrate that the *sine qua non* of that development is not large-scale help from outside but, primarily, that nations, however poor, should achieve a certain internal equilibrium, should assume awareness of their identity, of their own particular

genius. Now it seems that in a bi-polar organization of the
world, such as is implicit in the idea of a 'third world', this
internal equilibrium is in constant jeopardy. The coexistence,
even if peaceful, of two camps means that economically weak
nations become the stake in conflicts whose range is far wider
than themselves, but which affect them profoundly and painfully.
It is surely not necessary to emphasize this obvious and immediate aspect of the problem, which alone would justify the quest
for a political neutralism strong enough to discourage useless and
ruinous passions, and at the same time for an international order
other than dichotomous. But we must above all stress certain
even more disastrous effects of the 'third world' concept, which
prevents us from grasping the diversity of the problems and consequently of their solution. So long as we fail to take into
account and to respect this diversity, any form of aid will consist
merely of rival methods and influences forcibly imposed, pre-
venting the countries we are supposedly helping from discovering themselves, from remaining themselves, or learning the
indispensable lesson from their own past. These restrictions,
superficial or deep-rooted, explain those excessive nationalist
feelings which are the most serious obstacle to internal equilibrium and, paradoxically, to economic progress.

But in actual fact the bi-polar concept of the world is already
out of date. If the Third World idea is spreading, its reality
vanishes, even though some thinkers still cling to the notion like
benighted travellers on a false trail. For China, among others,
adds a complication to this over-simplified geographical concept.

One of China's rulers, recently, turned to a visitor and asked
him with some curiosity, 'What do you mean by the "third
world"?'

'The "third world" means the under-developed countries.'

'Then can China form part of it?'

'No, for China is in the Communist camp.'

'Then cannot an uncommitted country, even if it is rich, belong to the Third World?'

'......'

Receiving no satisfactory answer, he smiled as though with relief. The ambiguous character of this Third World offers China her opportunity. It allows some fine strategy. Thus China follows her own path. She urges each nation to be its individual self, while we in the West, to satisfy our own passions or to simplify our arguments, put into the same category India and Africa, Burma and Brazil, Cambodia and the Congo . . .

Some day the time will come for real remedies, if men can survive this monstrous contest, the stake for which is that Third World whose diversity is gradually assuming shape, flexibility and organization, in terms of realities which seem to go beyond immediate awareness.

3 - Synthesis

To understand in their general lines the differences between China and 'Europe', it is not enough to go back to the biological origins of languages, to examine the workings of technologies, to assess unconscious factors or to compare ways of thought, both popular and learned; one needs to form a dynamic picture of the whole thing, to see how those immense collective entities, China and 'Europe', function, to find out what are the feelings powerful enough to animate entire civilizations, their reasons for belief and action: an almost superhuman task, in which the danger of generalizing is only too apparent.

The comparative analysis which has been used hitherto has been confined to a few probings on points chosen for their suggestive value. The historical interpretation which follows can only be a kind of illustration of these. It will no doubt neglect a number of disciplines and forget the results of certain others, but it must be undertaken, for incalculable forces have now come into play whose power must inevitably increase.

Today, China has shut herself off completely[1], and wears an unfriendly look. An order reigns there, such as past tyrants never dreamed of. The indoctrination of her citizens implies, over and above conformity of behaviour, conformity of feeling, a proselytic revolution impatient to convert the world. Only the future will assess the extent of this emotional ambition which is finding an echo outside China in those countries, new or old, where the demand for 'liberation' is growing apace, determining their politics, dominating their economy and their

[1] In 1964 in China foreigners were fewer than 1 per million of the population.

whole future. This passion is said to be a result of progress. But it is not only provoked by violence or injustice, by the remembrance of colonial oppression, still less by the desire for wealth or the resentment of poverty; it is first and foremost a mystique, in the deepest and truest sense of the word, that is to say the sense of unity recovered, or suddenly discovered.

This observation seems paramount. In order to confirm it fully the historian should have at his disposal the most complete data, both on events and on the social and psychological phenomena these represent. He should write history as a psychologist. Are we not familiar today with the concept of psychological warfare? Collective as well as individual experiences would be taken into account. The biography of Mao Tse-tung is indispensable for the understanding of the People's Republic; but it would mean nothing without the 'biography' of the whole Chinese people. For history of this sort should grasp the basic relations between the individual and the community, each seeking self-realisation by means of the other.

The hypothesis on which we shall now base our argument does not claim to offer any universal law of human development—far from it—but it is founded on observations which it appears to confirm.

Collective psychology must obviously be something more than the study of the fleeting elements of mass consciousness which affect the human atom lost amid the impermanent crowd. It must examine all the enduring, interdependent structures which enfold each individual like the skins of an onion: family, class, nation, civilization, humanity itself, each endowed with a more or less determined amount of physical space. These collective entities are held to be unconscious, but no doubt they are more or less closely reflected in the individual, that final and unique centre of consciousness. Can this reflection be dissociated from the individual consciousness? To accept this abstraction would be to anticipate scrupulous research and risk reverting to organicist theories, to a certain psychological realism, which are said to be outmoded or dangerous. But let us remember, this is only a 'working hypothesis'.

The collective being, then, has a more or less clearly defined physical body: the house, the province, the native land, the continent or the planet in which its psyche dwells. Its collective ego has been somewhat neglected, no doubt because its consciousness is so faint that it seems more like unconsciousness. But could one not extend to the collective entity that which introspection reveals within the individual: relations with the material world, a sense of action, of responsibility, of commitment, alienation, a mystique, or the notion of social time: the relative enduringness of family, nation and so on?... Such might be the object of that 'structural psychology' we have already referred to. The study of the relation between the physical and psychological aspects of the collective entity suggests interesting parallels with the individual: the growth of the body, a period of physical formation, is that of an awakening of consciousness prior to adulthood, which in turn involves deeper reflective processes. Is it not remarkable that those nations endowed by nature with a limited insular space—England and Japan for instance—were quicker to achieve a certain inward awareness, a certain organic density, reflected in something proud and self-confident in the individual (which however does not preclude imperialist ambitions)? The collective being, so long as the space wherein it dwells is threatened, or has the chance to expand, is possessed by a will to power, an emotional unconsciousness which may result in violence. When its territorial ambitions are checked by history or geography, and its area is reduced to a size proportionate to its powers, the collective being turns inward and seeks something else, it increases its inner reflection. France loses her territorial empire, and straightway sets to cleaning her blackened capital! Beyond nationalities there lies the vast realm of civilizations, whose will to conquest or expansion over the whole earth is projected in each individual, together with an obscure sense of loathing for the rival civilization, of resentment for its transcendence and a passionate resolve to absorb or suppress it.

A comparison between collective and individual phenomena

and a study of their interaction might shed interesting light on the problem. They seem sufficiently alike in nature and behaviour for the same laws of consciousness to seem applicable in both cases. Indeed, the same upward-driving force seems to animate them both.

The effects of time and space have brought mankind, in two million years, from the prehistoric 'homo habilis' to that 'Great Society' which seems so imminent that it has already inspired philosophies, fed ideologies, inflamed ambitions and mystiques, all of them world-embracing. This undoubtedly represents an upward movement of man's consciousness.

Once this is admitted, three rules might be assumed: the first is that consciousness must project itself on centres, whether sparks, stars or sun, luminous condensations surrounded by the 'infinite spaces' of unconsciousness, constellations from which the individual and his various groupings, from the family to the whole of mankind, take their bearings. The second is that consciousness is inseparable from action: its centre must coincide with some object that can be modified, or else it will grow faint. This would be the 'praxis' of individuals and of collective beings, the nucleus, perhaps, of the 'spiritual energy' in which freedom of action consists, and whose irresistible movement is reflected in the upward trend of the human consciousness. Could one not imagine a 'nuclear' study, in which organic masses and their movements would yield their secret, in some degree, to science, according to methods akin to those of nuclear physics? Bergson imagined a kind of psychological atomism, the theory of which may be revived; and it has been said that physics is becoming the study of organizations, which suggests its kinship with biology, psychology and sociology.

The third rule would be that consciousness manifests itself as an effort to study oneself, to see oneself from outside. Thus the individual seeks to escape from the groupings that envelop him. He only becomes aware of his family, of his country, by going outside them; he questions his mirror; he craves to see the earth from the moon! Since he cannot break free from his too solid body, compact of unconsciousness, his introspection seeks in mysticism or metaphysics the right to escape from it for a while.

The collective being, however, sees its physical body fastened firmly in space, cannot move away nor see itself from outside. Thus, though a blind mass of unconsciousness, it seeks to break out of its limits, to increase in size. It presses confusedly on its frontiers, while within its organization there develop points of consciousness, some of which might by analogy be described as collective mysticism or metaphysics.

On this hypothesis, we might express the general upward trend of consciousness as follows:

In primitive times, a single man in whom the collective ideal is concentrated—chief, king, prophet, sage or saint—stands above the herd. As the latter becomes organized, a greater number of individuals can be distinguished. With the earliest civilizations, society becomes diversified at an increased rhythm. The individual self takes on consistency, breaks away from blind acceptance of the general will, inscribes his advantages on the tables of law. This is the dawn of individual liberties. The personal universe widens, enriched with numerous new points of consciousness. The release of an increasing number of individuals requires a constant adaptation of the social body, on pain of losing its cohesion. For the emergence of the individual is a threat of anarchy unless some collective ideal (which we may for convenience's sake call a *symbol* to distinguish it from the personal ideal) should prove powerful enough to transcend the individual self.

The rise of collective consciousness follows a similar rhythm. One group embodying a 'symbol' rises above the others, gathers them about it and expands. With civilization, these 'symbols' multiply, acquire consistency, until they take on so contagious, or so exemplary, a value as to reinforce, or transcend, material power in the conquest of space. This process means the digestion, the assimilation, the 'acculturation' of symbols, in step with the expansion of the civilized world, while the selfish interest of collective entities such as class, nation and so on threaten that world's internal cohesion . . .

So might the elements of that kaleidoscope be roughly sketched in which appear the unforeseen patterns of history.

The rise, the apogee and the decline of empires may be interpreted by the progressive development, harmonization and conflict of individual and collective consciousnesses. Thus Montesquieu explains that '. . . the Romans conquered all nations by their maxims [symbols] but when they had achieved this end they had to change their government, and maxims contradicting the previous ones, used by this new government, brought about their fall from greatness.'[1]

Already Greece had vanished through having given freedom to only one man out of nine, or for having believed, like Florence, that 'Art could exercise over life that unique, unlimited sway that Science claims today.'[2]

Their symbols were unequally distributed, or were inadequate. Closer to our own day the Renaissance, for all its sublimely intelligent princes and artists of genius, witnessed a high degree of immorality, and faith, hitherto a 'symbol' of cohesion, was irrecoverably shaken. The physical universe expanded. Europe was saved, however, for by the 17th century a new 'symbol' of civilization rose in its firmament; that of 'Progress'. This exciting projection of the collective consciousness rises while scientific discoveries, with political, economic and social inventions are made and, assembled into doctrines—of State control or liberalism—which are today being subjected to experiment by the nations. But this movement is drawing to a close, or at any rate the idea of progress is dwindling, excites less enthusiasm. We have seen, we still see, too many examples of brutality, injustice, servitude and misery against which progress is powerless; these emphasize the limitations of science and make us turn elsewhere. The more the individual enjoys the fruits of progress, the more his universe expands and therefore loosens, the less he is satisfied. Burdened with desires, centred on self, he yearns for

[1] Montesquieu, *Les Considérations*, ch. XVIII, 1734.
[2] Brunetière, *Questions actuelles*, 1907.

'somewhere to see himself from', while his civilization seeks to spread still further. Gradually there has emerged the ideal of 'development', a new panacea but an uncertain beacon: despite the anguished fear that once hunger, ignorance and disease have been suppressed in the world there may be nothing left but tumult and regression, the theory of 'development' seeks to re-habilitate progress, to broaden it until it consists in man himself rather than in his works. Its present outcome is 'cooperation', a symbol which as yet has spun only that thin and fragile thread: the hope of a change within man, of inner progress! Thinkers today are endeavouring to clarify this concept. Envisaging new infinities, they suggest that the biological phase of human evolution must be followed by a psychological one, to which the history of civilizations would form a sort of prelude. Will such a prospect be enough to overcome self-seeking, to arouse men's consciousness in the 'West', which is now wholly threatened since, with the loss of its universal faith, its symbols of liberty, justice and progress are spread unequally or else still limited to material objectives. Mounier forecasts that 'absurdity and despair will reign until the Western consciousness, overcoming its present crisis, shall have recovered a new vital impulse and a new human equilibrium.'

In any case, the present crisis is that of the whole world, for 'Europe' has carried it into all parts of the globe, including China.

But China, although obeying the same upward drive, has not the same symbols. The personal universe of the Chinese, although it has constantly gained in richness and consistency, seems less drawn than ours to extremes of isolation and abstraction. China's constellations of collective ideals—or symbols—transcending the personal self, have upheld through all its crisis the oldest of living civilizations. In the course of four thousand years the torch has been handed on through twenty-three dynasties. The Heavenly throne has always survived from one revolution to the next, often through tidal waves of popular feeling. Through fire and brimstone, through phases of decadence, destruction and revival, the Phoenix of the Chinese Chosen People has alighted on successive capital cities. While the 'West' was shifting from Athens to Rome, from Byzantium to Paris, London, Moscow and Washington, China, in the course of time, moved from An Yang to Peking, by way of Lo-Yang, Si-An, Chang-An, Cheng-Tu, Nanking, Hang-Chou, Canton . . . Kingdoms were conquered, were federated or fused, by force, by diplomacy or by contagious example: thus was gradually built up the 'Middle Kingdom'. We may wonder whether the secret of China's perenniality does not in fact lie in the nature of her personal ideals, which survive the shocks of history because they fit in better than ours do with collective symbols, whether those of family, state or the entire civilization. In this light, the Taiwan crisis reveals gleams of solidarity which entirely transcend the situation.

The hope of every Chinese, one might say of every man of the Far East, is manifest today. And the stability of these collective ideals would, it seems, result from their interconnection, their convergence and finally the balance they maintain with the individual ideals.

In the West, unrepentant individualism, together with short-sighted rationalism, have destroyed certain essential attitudes of loyalty and subordination. When faith has bound us together for a long time there is harmony between the extreme poles of our consciousness. The Christian believes that man is linked to God. But already Calvin had exclaimed, at the hour of crisis:

'Our feebleness is such that unless the Scriptures direct us to seek God, we forthwith drift away from Him . . .'

It is at this time that science and progress, which remain purely intellectual ventures unless they deliberately seek to be humanist or humanitarian, transcending selfish aims, bear us to the edge of that abyss of destruction, from which we turn away terrified, bewildered, seeking other horizons.

China exerts her vitality otherwise. The Chinese believe man linked not to God but to the universe. Within the 'heavenly realm', as in some immense church, the mass of the faithful forgather, convinced that no valid ideal exists outside it; conscious of its contradictions but also of its harmonies, familiar with its rites, decorating its countless chapels, steeped in its temporal and spiritual light, sometimes as oblivious of self as were the sculptors of our cathedrals, the Chinese believer proceeds with patience and with passion to the slow building-up of this world beneath heaven. And the crises undergone during its growth are so many dangerous intervals, after which balance is restored.

According to Zenker, the following explains how and why China, some two thousand years ago, overcame a grave peril in her history, 'The situation of China in the Chou period might have been enough to bring about the disappearance of State and nation, and to bury Chinese culture under their ruins, as had formerly happened to the Sumerian and Assyrian civilizations. This catastrophe was avoided, thanks to the principles of social morality which anonymous philosophers had developed in prehistoric times and which had become permanently incorporated, firstly into popular religion, and secondly into the spiritual life of the ruling classes. It is easy to understand that the great and vital crisis of the Chinese people in the first thousand years B.C. could not be surmounted through political cunning or legal methods, nor by force, but that only the moral resurgence of the whole people could solve the problem. If the prophets of this recovery and revival were listened to and understood by the people, if the seed they sowed did not fall on stony ground, this was due to the fruitful influence of this ancient philosophy . . . Thus the period of profound misery through which the Chinese people lived under the Chous proved to be the school of a brilliant renascence and the classical period of Chinese literature and philosophy.'[1]

There might seem to be some analogy here with present-day China. For its crisis, we must remember, is not solely due to 'Europe'. At the time when we first made contact with the

[1] Zenker, *Histoire de la Philosophie Chinoise*. Payot, 1932.

Chinese world it already stretched, as we have seen, over vast
territories, its frontiers (like Europe's in the 16th century) were
bursting asunder, and its dimensions were so great, its internal
variations so marked, that the symbols of its civilization had begun to decline. The individual self was emerging, while the
guiding lights were dimmed by stages—the highest first—as the
tide of anarchy rose. The sanctuary of the family was still secure
and still impressive, but it had begun to show cracks. The up-
surge of egotistic demands from feudal warlords and from a
numerous élite rent asunder the overgrown social body. China
was on the eve of one of those great waves of collective emotion
that mark her history, and which dialectical materialism has not
yet been able to explain. As we have also seen, the Taiping revolt (1860) was a symptom of this.

This was when, as if swooping down from another planet,
'Europe', at a stage in its own evolution marked by a parallel
decline in its supreme ideals and torn by national rivalries at the
primary level of a contest for power, suddenly introduced into
China, in the first place, those violent motivations which everywhere have their repercussions on the individual. The Chinese,
who had known neither the fascination of civil liberties, nor
that of art for art's sake, nor that of science, nor the intense
aspiration towards unlimited material progress, were thus
introduced to unfamiliar wealth and an unfamiliar disquiet.
Among the élite, the sudden conjunction of the Chinese and
'Western' concepts of personal life brought about an intensifica-
tion of individualism, to the point of auto-intoxication. The
State began to fall apart, while the peasantry drifted, as though
on a makeshift raft, amid a storm of purely indigenous origin
which our intervention, ever since the Taiping revolt, has
doubtless prolonged and aggravated.

Words are inadequate to describe the state of this cradle of
civilization in the first half of the present century. It displays the
crazy confusion of an empire in decline. The ever-growing
masses of the people endured famines. Brutal soldiers ravaged
the countryside, plundering, burning and slaughtering. After
each disaster the peasant would rebuild his walls, pick up his

charred roof-tiles and start sowing again, borrowing seed at 12 per cent per month, selling all he possessed, even his children, and leaving his dead unburied in the streets. And yet his spirit was unconquered. His capacity for happiness fastened on to the slightest crack in the rock face. If a somewhat more generous harvest enabled him to buy some badly-needed garment, the whole village would rejoice. But the soldiers came back. The warlords, who were as vain, hypocritical and cruel as they were cowardly, ambitious and licentious, took possession of public property and carried on their intrigues in an atmosphere of feasting and bargaining, treachery and murder. As for the 'Europeanized' élite, they cast about, in the depths of their disillusion, for desperate remedies and reforms, or else concerned themselves with building up fabulous fortunes, still for their own families.

This was when Chinese Communism was born. Now that we are trying to understand the causes of the Sino-Soviet dispute and the nature of divergences which have today become manifest, we must take into account the fact that the political, economic and social situation of Tsarist Russia had little in common with the China of Sun Yat-sen. But this provides only a partial explanation. We might add that there are permanent differences of mentality between the Russian worker and intellectual on the one hand, and the Chinese peasant and thinker on the other. Is this sufficient to show us that the two great political movements are not of the same order? Between the whole of 'Europe' and China, between two universalist cultures, two civilizations considered in their entirety, there lies the source of a global misunderstanding, the cause of a revolution which seems of a wholly new essence.

The Russian Revolution, at the start, only sought to remedy a social evil within 'Europe', with the help of European formulae. If the crisis was indeed a crisis of 'European' civilization, Russia did not solve it. For while putting science at the service of man, she made man the object rather than the subject of her conception of the universe.

The Chinese Revolution is unquestionably a political, economic and social one, but above all a moral revolution, and therefore, as we have summed it up, a revulsive crisis. For it is also a crisis in China's civilization which must be surmounted: an internal crisis in the first place, but aggravated by 'Europe' to the extent of requiring, in part, European solutions. Civilization, we have said, is not only a social phenomenon but a mental and spiritual one as well. How can one imagine that the demoralization and decadence of the Chinese world could have been checked—even after the buyers and sellers had been driven from the temple with the fury of a blood-bath—by the proud doctrines of a purely scientific materialism? Something else was needed, and the supreme ideal of the 'Chinese church' had to be saved. The conformity of feeling required by and explained by the fervour of present-day China recalls, some say, our own Reformation. The People's Republic of China, like Geneva in 1550, does not give the impression of a police state or a dictatorship. But mutual censorship, the constant watch kept there over the conduct of 'believers' not to judge them, but to warn them, gently and 'humanely'—weave so subtle a network that no secret glance goes unchecked, while the savoury smell of some over-rich dish is promptly denounced to the local authority.

How can one try in a few lines to analyse doctrines so vast, and facts so complex? History will outline and clarify the differences, for sooner or later reality pierces through the screen of alliances and conflicts. Meanwhile, however, it is possible to distinguish certain ideas.

Marxism is a dynamic conception of the world. It seeks to give a rational and scientific explanation of history. Its origins lie deep in the European consciousness; its construction involves special intellectual instruments and a highly specialized knowledge. It is constantly concerned with the opposition between matter and mind, which is the source of all philosophic systems based on contradictions—Marxist or otherwise—from Heraclitus to Hegel and to our own day, which explain evolution as the struggle of life against matter. The Marxist interpretation of history bases itself on eras which it defines by the evolution of material techniques and the corresponding stages of the mind's knowledge of the outside world. It professes to be a scientific form of sociology, and yet it never succeeds in penetrating the mystery of cultures, a complex phenomenon, wholly psychological in character, which defines periods and yet transcends them. Dare one suggest that there may exist between man and nature, just as between man and man, as many harmonies as contradictions? China's experience might confirm this. And could one not construct systems of ideas parallel to dialectical materialism, such as for instance a psychological dialectic, to explain cultures?

Bergson, meanwhile, says, 'The ideas we form about things—the world of ideas—are only the real, material world expressed and reflected in men's minds, that is to say they are built up on a basis of practice, and from active contact with the outside world, through a complex process *in which all forms of culture are included.*' But he does not go further. Thus culture, an evident fact of mind, a phenomenon of consciousness and not of knowledge, is still unexplained by European thought. Marxist sociology, politics or economy, expressions of that thought, come up against this hitherto insuperable obstacle. If culture does indeed consist of man's sensibility, educated, organized and constructed throughout different periods of time, does it not derive from the contact of mind with human nature as much as with physical nature? And is it not an even more irrational undertaking to try to conquer and dominate human nature at the same time as physical nature?

Liberalism is opposed to Marxism, and yet the ideal of personal freedom is central to both—remember the dogma of the withering-away of the State—and this is equally unsatisfying to the Chinese mind; indeed, far more dangerous in China's view, at this stage of history. This explains in part China's choice, and the disturbing and apparently unjust violence of her hostility to the United States, the most powerful and dynamic champion of individual freedom. Marxism also has this in view, and pro-

mises the fulfilment of the individual through the suppression
of various ties, those of family, class and State; but this theore-
tical prospect is being gradually contradicted in Russia itself
by the facts.

One of the attractions of Marxism for the Chinese is that it
slows down this movement of individual liberation and, moreover, shows a certain respect for cultures which although unexplained are too powerful to be ignored. Liberalism is less conscious of them, and does not seek to canalize cultural forces,
which in any case is impossible according to its view, since culture is the quintessence of liberty. Individual liberty, brought
about by a series of successive adaptations to experience and at
the cost of enormous struggles and sacrifices, means that the
human personality, in the West, wears an aura of liberties and
dignities which are the hope of humanity, the charter of the
Rights of Man, the extreme point of consciousness to be preserved at all costs since it holds in germ all other liberties, all
imaginable forms of human progress. Outside this, there is nothing but regression, temporary or permanent. But our collective ties, up to and including that of civilization, have been
weakened, and for this reason our personal liberties are in
danger. The 'European' world has been stretched till it is almost
coextensive with the planet, but its symbols are inadequate, and
the tide of egotism is rising.

Liberty, that 'gift of civilization' as Malinowsky called it,
cannot be entirely concentrated on the individual without
endangering the collective being. It must be distributed in
stages, by successive compromises, from top to bottom of the
edifice of mankind. It is a truism to say that liberty cannot be
entirely lodged in the State without jeopardizing the individual,
nor entirely in the individual without weakening the State, and
indeed the whole of civilization. The 'liberation' of China, its
total emancipation from all accepted rules of international law,
suppresses individual liberties or dims them, transcending personal consciousness. This liberation also threatens world cohesion.

Whether instinctive, willingly accepted or imposed by
authority, this narrowing of personal liberties is a fact sufficiently

evident in China to explain how today, drawn together by a collective emotion, by the mystique of unity regained, that country can experience and accept this sort of concentrated form of liberty at the summit of the social edifice. But this passion is far from being simple. It is an unconscious mingling of hope and anger, a concentration on two-faced 'symbols' through which the Chinese world is being reorganized and strengthened while at the same time asserting its will to expansion.

China's will is stronger than ever before. She has shaken off her passivity and is mobilizing men, minds and hearts in order to win the whole world by persuasion. This has hitherto been chiefly in self-defence, but ominous signs are already appearing: fostering passions is a well-known psychological method, too effective not to be perilous.

The scale of wars has kept pace with the development of weapons: the bow, the sword, gunpowder, and now the atomic bomb. With each invention, the renewal of conflict demands and destroys more people and more things. Tribal contests, clashes between populations, religious wars, international conflicts are now being succeeded by wars between civilizations . . . This is the dark side of the emergence of consciousness. And how can one imagine that any form of disarmament, be it sudden or gradual, could permanently obliterate the apocalyptic nightmare glimpsed by us all today? Passion is gaining hold of men, who are still stirred by atavistic impulses in modern disguise: old, pathetic instincts of hatred which refuse to be allayed before having sought unbridled release at whatever cost. While terror holds the world in uneasy equilibrium, awareness of these realities is beginning to appear. Men talk of peace, but as yet only timidly: not, yet, of that 'Great Peace' of which the Chinese have long cherished the symbol. 'T'ai Ping'[1] was the emblem of their revolt in the 19th century. But China herself is mobilizing, and nothing less than atomic weapons would serve for

---

[1] T'ai Ping .. Great Peace.

what she seeks to defend. China has often despised violence and arms; today she honours her warriors. Strategists in every country have begun to be influenced by China's warlike stance. We used to talk about the Yellow Peril; today the Chinese, if they were racists, would talk about the White Peril. But the idea that is mobilizing them is something that goes far beyond race. What they want is not so much the vital space that their demography demands, nor that men of a certain colour should survive, nor yet material well-being; but also, and above all, they are concerned to preserve their highest values, into which ours have begun to infiltrate, and this is what provokes their alarum which echoes right into the depths of the African forest: 'Down with imperialism!' But what imperialism? 'Down with colonialism!' But whose? The dominance of comfort, of capital, of individual liberty, of technique, of science, or else that of 'European' civilization? This powerful ferment of passion is too concentrated, too violent to allow of analysis. None the less it is, and it must be, the object of our first effort towards disarmament, the systematic cooling-down of hate, without which the 'Great Peace' seems likely to achieve nothing but the disintegration of all those things through which it might have asserted itself. If the atomic bomb is already impelling the nations to settle their differences, if it is imposing mutual respect on régimes which only yesterday vowed one another's destruction, it can and must make possible the survival and, as far as possible, the cooperation of systems of values even more alien and profoundly different, until they find the common point of the collective ideal and its harmony in the human personality. That is the core of the problem, the real 'passion' of humanity, its torment, the 'way' towards a new consciousness or towards ruin. This conflict goes beyond the bounds of temporal power and bears no relation to political systems. The quest for 'liberation' has really nothing to do with megatonic stocks; and yet it deserves as much attention as if it already wielded nuclear power; it yearns for it and must have it some day, unless the world understands and accepts the intense and legitimate impulse whence it draws its strength.

For China is not solely mobilized by her will to survive. She is also experiencing the excitement of anticipated happiness. And this is the primary message she is seeking to send out to all the 'under-developed' nations of the earth, and which some seem to understand. What is this revolution, what is its hope? Nothing less than the construction of a new Church, commensurate with all mankind. To win the whole world! An extravagant ambition perhaps, but it can and must awaken profound echoes within our own hearts; for we are familiar with it, we still cherish it unconsciously, though our own ideals have become inadequate. China has joined 'Europe'—Communist, capitalist and Christian Europe—in seeking the unity and happiness of mankind: and she intends to forestall Europe. Whereas Europe has glimpsed the possibility of man's changing, China is changing man: she has inaugurated the reign of virtues which, by force and by persuasion, have prevailed, and whose example has already proved contagious. 'I don't intend,' the Chinese seems to say, 'to barter my identity for an easy chair, but I will make total abdication of my personal freedom provided man can go on believing in himself and respecting himself.'

This kind of totalitarianism is unlike any other. Beyond the State, it is also that of a civilization concerned with the whole of mankind. And so while others have not passed the stage of preaching the sharing-out of material wealth and the freeing of the individual solely by means of economic production and distribution, the Chinese revolution is not 'for the sake of man', it is 'within man'. A revolution within man! Is not that what we long for, while the great powerhouses rise up all over the globe and megatonic stocks pile up at danger-spots? Our dissatisfaction is growing. We are well aware that progress must affect man, and no longer only his works. China answers in her own fashion. But where is progress, we may say, if liberty is sacrificed? Virtue under compulsion is only partial virtue, a makeshift, a frightening short-cut. No matter; China has made a start. And there is no other way, if liberty is to be saved, than to awaken that new consciousness, the thirst for progress or for a change of heart which would justify any effort and any sacrifice. There is no other way, save to allay this frantic instinct for self-defence, so that the Chinese personality, so rich, yet today wholly swayed by that passion, should some day regain its peace.

Explosive hatred must be unprimed! On the one hand, China is conscious of over a century of humiliations; on the other, centuries of success have fostered our own self-assurance. Loathing, scorn and repulsion are quick to take root on both sides by a sort of deep-seated instinctive will to resist 'the other', and at the same time a resolve to defend and propagate to the last, by all means in our power, what we know, and have secured and realized. Any war on this plane is now suicide, for mankind is one.

While we offered care, food and instruction to the peoples of Africa and Asia, China made their representatives at Bandung, in 1955, sign a resolution against 'cultural oppression', thus showing that an active phase had begun in that war which is neither 'cold' nor 'hot' but invisible, as are the fears which it arouses in the threatened cultures, clinging passionately to life.

At Peking in 1960 China, through the voice of her six thousand delegates, expressed her 'resolute opposition to the reactionary ideas of so-called Western civilization, and its professed slogan Liberty, Equality, Fraternity . . . her will to crush the efforts of the Imperialists . . . her violent condemnation of American imperialism, the greatest enemy of all the countries in the world . . . her intention of carrying the cultural revolution to the highest level . . .'[1]

And at Algiers in 1964 China declared that 'to require oppressed nations to coexist peacefully with Imperialism means condemning them to perpetual slavery. The fight against Imperialism and Colonialism is a life-and-death struggle. To assert that economic reconstruction is the primary task incumbent on the developing nations is a senseless line of argument.'[2]

We might see in this merely a straightforward Leninist picture of uninterrupted revolution. But there is something else to be

[1] Chinese Cultural Congress, June 1960. The turn of events in 1966 has brought new evidence of this determination.
[2] Speech by Mme Kuo Tchien, 23rd March 1964.

considered: Africa and Asia, China, India, the world of Arabs, Persians and Turks, immemorial and imperturbable currents whose richness transcends materialism and which lead forward to a future of peace or of chaos, according to whether men recognize, or fail to recognize, their reality and their strength.

China's language is clear. To answer her we need only call a halt to destruction. But what are we destroying? say the science-obsessed rationalist, the Manichean for whom there is this Third World oscillating between good and evil, or the idealist who envisages a free world in opposition to the enslaved world, yet who is ready enough to go off on a crusade against liberties which he does not recognize. Yes, there has been moral and psychological destruction of societies, great and small: African tribes, China, and ourselves. For no society can exist without traditions, without authenticity. And if the 'European' world today seems so overstretched that it is in danger of losing its collective ideals, these must be renewed as the old symbols grow faint in the great society, representing an imperfect way of life, the common characteristic of our worried humanism.

The devaluation of symbols, the loss of traditions, are not due solely to industrialization and material progress, but rather to the distension of our societies and to the confusion of styles, made uniform and neutralized by incessant intermingling. Must we then assume that such a process can be halted by a re-partitioning of humanity, so as to preclude the flow of influences and allow provincialisms to revive? One might as well seek to stop the sun in its course! This irresistible movement can neither be interrupted nor confined nor controlled. But why should we not seek for fresh symbols, for values high enough to ensure that understanding between men, so dangerously lacking today? And why should not the respect for certain collective feelings at all levels contain incipient truth and hope? Those States which have recently entered into international political and economic life seek to safeguard for their future generations those aspects of knowledge which are not only their way of life, not only their particular form of humanism, but also their essential and prac-tical means of survival. That is the lesson China teaches.

And what is being done? Traditional wisdom is disappearing without any alternative being taught. Everywhere, and at every level, are destroyed—by neglect and with the best of intentions —the political, economic and moral 'motivations' of societies, great and small: from those of the smallest tribe to China's, and our own. And not only through the ravages due to exported alcohol, through violent and sensual films, connivance at corruption, the crazy ugliness of certain forms of art—fruit of heady liberty, 'grapes of wrath'—but also through the technical 'expert' who fails to understand Africa's moral code, the statistician for whom Buddhism is just another obstacle to economic development, the politician eager to apply his theories, or the proud humanist condemning the Chinese script to relatively rapid extinction.

The Chinese Revolution calls itself a cultural one. We should ponder the term and consider China's agonizing efforts to define her 'new culture', which suggest a sea-captain's dramatic order to fling some precious cargo overboard, clearing the deck before a battle or a storm. Civilization and culture belong to the realm of mind. These pages have sought to show that they are the fundamental issue and that we shall have no real dialogue with China or many other countries, no real development and above all no co-operation without full awareness of this and the emergence of a corresponding ideal, which alone will allow true communication between men.

We must then return to Montesquieu and find those 'maxims' which will guide each and all of us towards unity, saying with him, with all the power of his hidden irony, 'Certain petty minds have exaggerated the injustice we do the Africans; for if it were such as they have described it, would it not have occurred to the Princes of Europe, who make so many useless agreements amongst themselves, to make a general one in favour of pity and mercy?'[1]

In favour, we might add today, of all forms of culture, of all those techniques, of all the families, groups, nations, arts, thoughts and feelings in which every individual and every

[1] Montesquie, *Esprit des Lois*, XV. 5, 1748.

collective being find their unity, their cohesion and their irreplaceable dignity. Respect for rights and duties, for liberty and for fraternity of cultures. This complex thing, whose mystery is as impenetrable as that of the inner self, deserves as much liberty and protection as does the individual, for the two are inseparable. We have our Declaration of Human Rights, we have made an attempt to write down a Charter, but the respect for human cultures remains a dead letter, with no other moral implication than an exchange of floral tributes. The world of cultures has, before our eyes, become a jungle: the flocks are scattered . . . today the dragon of China awakes once more from its telluric slumber, breathing flames and wreathed in cloud, fascinated by this glittering pearl, the globe, where Heaven reflects its ever-changing patterns.

On the evening after the battle of Valmy, when a people's army had checked a coalition of kings, Goethe foresaw that the blue blood of the aristocracy had run dry and that a new dawn was breaking over humanity. Shall we again have to wait for an event of this order, and hear, by some deserted mill, after battle the irresistible strains of a people's hymn proclaiming that the pride and arrogance of the technocrats have been brought low, that 'Western' rationalism is to be swept away by 'continents on the march towards us, with their vast riches and their contempt'?[1] This would come through a failure to see that between the individual and the universal there lies something without which the human machine breaks down. This is what China says; she must be listened to.

Bonaparte, leaving for Egypt, took scientists along with him . . . in order to see himself from outside, as we must do. A dead, mysterious civilization had looked down, from the top of its pyramids, on the soldiers of the French Republic. China, as old as Egypt was, but throbbing with life, is speaking. Surely it is imperative to overcome the loathing of one civilization for another, and for all the thinkers of the world to unite in listening to her. It is high time for us to seek by every possible means to ensure the stability and continuity essential for a firmly based

[1] Mounier.

peace and the inwardness which will enable us to pay heed to humbler, almost vanished ways of life, so as to prevent the spread over the whole face of the earth of an industrialized humanity, tormented by its own future!

Democracy and socialism have given rise to exemplary virtues, but there are others for lack of which peace will remain in jeopardy. Is the respect of values to be the sole prerogative of totalitarian states because free men shall have failed in their duty? Virtue without freedom is the strength of wars; freedom without virtue, the weakness of peace. The time appears to have come for a virtue freely assumed. It would prove irresistible.

4 - *Eighth letter*

My dear T'ang-lin,

When you telephoned, I did not recognize your voice, and for a few moments you made game of my perplexity. An hour later, I was with you again; your features, I thought, had hardened somewhat in ten years, your gaze seemed more piercing and as if it were riveted within itself. I felt you to be totally committed: to Communism, no doubt, but even more to China . . . a man from your remotest dynasties! During that single day, while we were alone together, I tried to guess what had happened within you.

In Paris, as though crushed by the shop windows' limitless display of articles and products, you said in a low, rapid whisper, 'China will have to wait a long time.' Towards noon we went at random into a crowded restaurant. We found seats at a table by a window, where noisy workmen were hurriedly finishing their meal. I cannot remember what we said, but two things have remained in my memory: I asked you if in China the press of the 'free world' reached you. You answered, 'Yes, but I've no desire to read it.' Then, *à propos* of Russian 'imperialism', you opened questioning eyes, as if your fine armour had been momentarily pierced. And then you left again.

That yesterday is long past already! Many years will go by . . . and silence.

In these letters I have tried to forget politics and above all the language of politics. Having seen you again, I can better understand your clenched teeth and fists, your mind in arms against external and internal threats. Imperialism and colonialism, those targets for China's unremitting attacks. What misunderstandings!

I saw your intense joy at feeling that your country was now
sheltered from the contagion of 'Europe', that Shanghai had
suddenly become a Chinese city—the longest bar in the world
standing deserted! If one of our great seaports, occupied for a
hundred years by a foreign power, had suddenly been restored
to us, I should have felt the same. Civilizations are fused and
forged in cities that form a continuous chain of crucibles, from
which at times an indescribable chaos flows. You have put an
end to that!

At Hankow in 1937—do you remember?—the railway had
just been bombarded. Over the crowded districts through
which we walked together there hung a confused feeling of that
Chinese xenophobia of which so much has been said. Gradually
I noticed that you wanted to walk on the other pavement . . .
and not to have me join you there. I suddenly felt a white man,
and alone! Now, as then, we follow parallel ways. And passions
are rising.

Already in those days political feeling seemed liable to set fire
to everything. You were discovering the true nature of nations,
you despaired at the idea of China being forced into that mould,
too narrow for her. There again, I can imagine your present
hope. China reunited! At what cost? Ah, I saw that you were
ready to pay, if necessary, with your whole being, with your
very life, in order to rebuild the crumbling structures. The
cultural revolution of which your orators now speak to eager
multitudes all over the world is under way everywhere. It is
surging up within us, despite our preoccupied minds and our
absent hearts. We must rediscover everything, and invent afresh.
For a motto, the King of Lu inscribed on his bath, 'New things,
more new things, forever new things!'

From the depths of my civilization I am writing these lines to
you, living so intensely in your own. Both are threatened. Indeed everything is threatened. Having 'known one another's
hearts', as you say in China, nothing can break our friendship.
But how can we prevent night from closing in around us, and
the passion of the antagonists from flaring up?

Postscript

SEVERAL years have elapsed since that last letter. Eventful years, marked in America, Africa and Asia by small revolutions, in India by great waves of hunger and by the rising tide of war in the direction of China. But the most important fact is that, as these pages had anticipated, China now has the bomb. In ten years she will have a large stock of bombs.

The world has never looked so much like (the comparison is Paul Valéry's) a modern fleet equipped with every sort of contraption, but lost in a dense fog settled on the sea. The messages that reach world leaders in this period of crisis are like those hasty notes which the commander gets from his subordinates in the thick of battle: half-truths, impermanent truths, to which action must be adjusted without delay by successive guesses. The time is no more when philosophers and poets guided the great; when Aristotle counselled Alexander, when Voltaire, 'King of Europe', visited kings. Poetry, it is said, is a moribund art, and philosophy is dying . . . The Western world, absorbed in what the poet Pierre Emmanuel calls its 'advertising euphoria', weighed down by the 'huge materialistic onslaught', no longer pays to poetry the passionate attention it once aroused . . . This inspiration, this tension between the psyche and its spiritual impulse, this inner life of each and every human collectivity, its identification with the destiny of its language, are still known in China today. As for philosophy, that 'love of wisdom' has become for us the business of professionals, of logicians, of lotus-eaters, who devote their energies to playing with difficult words and ideas—quite useless for men in a hurry.

The search for common truths needs time. Its findings are

generalities, of which nowadays we tend to be wary, for they are often hasty. And yet action must go on. And the fog thickens as the haven seems more distant, peace more problematic. The generalities to be found in the present work have not been reached in haste. Thirty years of observing and pondering over China in an effort to understand have led to convictions which many recent events have confirmed.

But the time has come to conclude, to sum up, to assemble these reflections. This could be done in one sentence, which would include, in the order of the book, the key words of each of its eight chapters. Thus:

China is undergoing a *revulsive crisis* (I) because this *Civiliza-tion-State* (II) in order to overcome its internal crisis and its *humiliation* (III) wants to *invent* (IV) and thus recover its *cohesion* (V) and its *inspiration* (VI) through its *educators* (VII) who mobilize it against *cultural oppression* (VIII)

Each chapter may have suggested what these words convey. Do the ideas contained in such a sentence, then, suffice to guide action, at all levels, and above all in politics?

To answer this I will limit myself to the two following con-clusions: the first is that the entry of China into world affairs is a philosophic problem; the second is that China is not a nation in the usual sense, but, as these pages tend to prove, a Civiliza-tion-State.

For China, the philosophic problem is today clearly set out. She lives with it, one might say. And if a certain love of wisdom were not ingrained as it is in her tradition, her present situation could by itself explain her total challenge of Western values. One must therefore understand on a philosophical level attitudes which otherwise would be unexplainable, one must observe the close relation between certain decisions and the common line of thought which inspires them. To illustrate this first point, here are two examples:

On October 16th 1964 China successfully carries out her first nuclear test. Next day the China News Agency broadcasts an official communiqué which ends thus, 'We are convinced that the atomic weapon, which after all is created by man, will be destroyed and certainly eliminated by man.' This has great significance. For the object is to destroy the myth created around this weapon in relation to man, at a time when the fear of this terrible invention holds men in a stalemate of terror which paralyses all true reflection. And when China declares that the atom bomb is but a paper tiger, she does not simply want to provoke or insult the Soviet Union or the United States, she wants to reaffirm a philosophy which is that 'the destiny of the world must be chosen by the peoples of the world, not by any weapon, be it an atomic one.'

The second example is from Chinese domestic politics. Tension at the top has recently occurred—serious enough for the outside world to realize it. This may be seen as the normal outcome of the country's intense military preparation. What is important is that one outcome of this tension in China (the cultural revolution and the continued pre-eminence of the civilian power) is officially justified by considerations identical with those, mentioned above, that referred to atomic weapons. War, say the Chinese, is not a matter for professionals, whose increasing technicity must not make us forget man. The Party declares that it cannot allow that essential element, man, to be relegated to second place. Thus the same idea dominates and commands what, otherwise, might be only a rivalry between leaders, teams and factions. Therein lies the whole difference. The force of this idea must be grasped, and that of the general mobilization at which it aims. It is both reassuring and disquieting: reassuring because China, in conformity with her long tradition, is concerned with cultural values and curtails the power of the military; disquieting because, at the same time, this mobilization suggests 'the ocean of the people in arms . . .'

Why the people in arms? The question haunts those who understand more and more that peace cannot be ensured without China taking a full part, somehow or other, permanently, in its elaboration. And naturally some hope for her admission into the United Nations Organization. This, too, implies a philosophical problem, for it includes the risk of an upheaval of the world Organization, of its structure, of its functions and even

of its very spirit. China is the most highly populated State in
the world. Her revolution seeks to call in question the very
foundations of the 1945 charter. True, she preaches government
by virtue, but at the same time she will not renounce war. As
long as China is conscious of the existence of certain threats, of
which this book may have given an idea, she will want to oppose
outside influences and ventures with the threatening power of
her people in arms. To subscribe to the Charter would, for her,
be tantamount to an implicit renunciation of her philosophy of
man. Her warlike attitude and her admission of the value of
war are frightening indeed. And it will clearly take a long time,
and many efforts to conciliate the divergent points of view at
this level. But that is far from being the only difficulty. China
will also question the Western concept of nationhood, She will
do this first, not only because she is Communist, not only
because she has bitter memories of her past relations with
Western nations. (As early as 1932, Mao Tse-tung had said,
'The League of Nations is a league of gangsters!') She will do so
because, as she herself tries to set up a multi-national order, she
observes that the idea of nationhood, in the West, is rapidly
changing. She will do so, finally, to fight the extravagant logic
of an institution which gives equal voice to the delegate of the
U.S.S.R. and to that of Nicaragua.

This brings us to the second main conclusion of this work,
which is that China is not a nation in the usual sense, and cannot
be considered as such.

When Machiavelli left his city-state of Florence to travel
across Europe, he discovered France, England, Spain, nation-
states of another dimension and another nature than the Italian
republics. He derived from this that view of political morality
which is still talked about today. Had he lived in our time, he
would have observed above modern nations the civilization-
states, either existing or in process of becoming. This is what
Europe will be tomorrow; we are conscious of it, we think
about it, we strive towards it. And this is what China has already
become, or has become once more. In the face of such realities,
Machiavelli would no doubt have drawn other lessons for the

Prince's conduct. For between Lorenzo the Magnificent and the King of France, in his day, there was as much difference as between, say, the present Queen of the Netherlands and Mao Tse-tung. The former represents a nation; with the latter, gradually and probably for a long period, a whole civilization identifies itself. This has little to do with the actual personality of Mao Tse-tung, who may be assessed, according to the usual standards, as a philosopher, poet, politician or simply as a man. It is one of the great sociological and political facts of this day that a whole civilization recognizes itself thus in one man, who incarnates the State at this level. This may not be sufficiently recognized as yet to dictate our policies. But it is inevitable that one day, not far off, as rivalries subside at the national level, confrontations will occur between larger entities made up of nations gradually united by the weight of their common past, in other words of their culture, in the sense given throughout these pages.

Already, while our growing anxiety accompanies the rise of the old alarums of war, intensified by atomic power, already a new consciousness is arising, a hope of some understanding at this level.

Thus, in the richest and most powerful nation in the world, in the nation which consequently, according to an historical and psychological law that seems ineluctable, should wish to conquer the world, since its present power allows it to conceive of such a conquest, in the United States itself,[1] voices are being raised: that of Professor George F. Kennan, who declares, 'Our country should not be asked and should not ask itself to shoulder the main burden of determining the political realities in any other country, and particularly not in [those] remote from our shores, from our culture, and from the experience of our people. This is not only not our business, but I don't think we can do it successfully.'

There is also the voice of Professor John K. Fairbank, 'We have been more conscious of our good intentions than of the humiliations imposed on the Chinese by unfavourable circum-

[1] In the Foreign Affairs Commission of the U.S. Senate, Feb-Mar. 1966.

225

stances . . . if because of Vietnam we today experience a crisis of consciousness, it is because during most of our history, we have believed ourselves to be morally superior . . .'

Such a recognition of the force of culture, the weight of history, the meaning of the present expansion and confrontation, marks the beginning of mutual respect and wisdom. It may be the dawn of new freedoms. A field is opening up here for our cautious but daring exploration: a field as vast as that already visited by a handful of cosmonauts.

Vietnam is at the centre of Chinese politics. China has contributed much to the culture and experience of its people. This reality must inspire all attempts to bring back peace to that lacerated peninsula. But to recognize this reality implies a philosophy of action which cannot be mere isolationism, but demands that capacity for 'living together', which in politics is called coexistence, with all its varied applications.

Beyond truces, beyond political agreements, if peace is to be established through co-operation, inspired not by out-of-date rivalries but by a collective symbol of sufficient strength, it is indispensable that the pride and the feeling of superiority which animate both the Chinese and ourselves should gradually disappear, making way for a better knowledge, a better mutual understanding. That is what this book is aiming at, in a modest way.

China has entered into our lives, never to leave. The Chinese rebel against this idea, and so do we. Perhaps, then, we shall have to resort to poetry and faith, even more than to science, in order that our techniques, our arts, our consciences, our thoughts and our passions may cease to conflict or to clash, and so that one day, perhaps, some harmony may assert itself.

Poissy Valmondois 1963–1966

Notes for further reading

Alain: *Propos*, Gallimard.

Arlington and Acton: *Famous Chinese Plays*, Vetch, 1937.

Barnett (A. Doak): *Communist China in Perspective*, Praeger, 1962.

Barthélemy-Madaule (Madeleine): *Bergson et Teilhard de Chardin*, du Seuil, 1963.

Carrère d'Encausse (Helène) et Stuart Schram: *Le Marxisme et l'Asie*, Armand Colin, 1965.

Chan: *A Source Book of Chinese Philosophy*, Princeton, 1963.

Collis (Maurice): *The First Holy One*, Faber & Faber, 1948.

Collotti-Pischel (Enrica): *La Révolution interrompue*, Julliard, 1964.

Conze (Edward): *Buddhism*, Bruno Cassirer, Oxford, 1951.

Creel (H.G.): *Chinese Thought, from Confucius to Mao Tse-tung*, Eyre and Spottiswood, 1954.

Demieville (Paul): *Anthologie de la Poésie Chinoise Classique*, Gallimard, 1962.

Descartes: *Discours de la Méthode*.

Dumont (René): *Révolution dans les Campagnes Chinoises*, du Seuil, 1957.

Eliot (T.S.): *Notes Towards the Definition of Culture*, Faber & Faber, 1948.

Fung Yu-lan: *A Short History of China*, Macmillan, New York. 1948.

Galbraith (John K.): *Economic Development in Perspective*, Harvard University Press, 1964.

Gernet (Jacques): *La Vie Quotidienne en Chine à la Veille de l'Invasion Mongole*, Hachette, 1959.

La Chine Ancienne, Presses Universitaires de France, 1964.

Granet (Marcel): *La Pensée Chinoise*, Albin Michel, 1950.

Etudes Sociologiques sur la Chine, Presses Universitaires de France, 1953.

Danses et Légendes de la Chine Ancienne, Alcan, 1925.

Fêtes et Chansons Anciennes de la Chine, Leroux, 1929.

Greene (Felix): *Awakened China*, Doubleday & Co., 1962.

Guillain (R.): *Dans Trente Ans La Chine*, le Seuil, 1965.

Gurvitch (George): *Morale Théorique et Science des Mœurs*, Presses Universitaires de France, 1948.

Halperin (Morton H.): *La Chine et la Bombe*, Calmann Lévy, 1965.

Han Su-Yin: *The Crippled Tree*, Jonathan Cape, 1965.

Hershey (John): *A Single Pebble*, Knopf, 1965.

Hsiao Ch'ien: *A Harp with a Thousand Strings*, Pilot Press, 1944.

Hung Wei-lien: *The Chinese Picture of Life*, Asia, 1931.

Jaspers (Karl): *La Bombe Atomique et l'Avenir de l'Homme*, Buchet Chastel, 1963.

Lasker (Bruno): *Les Peuples de l'Asie en Mouvement*, Payot, 1946.

Lattimore (O. & E.): *La Genèse de la Chine Moderne*, Payot, 1947.

le May (Reginald): *The Culture of South East Asia*, G. Allen and Unwin, 1954.

Lévi-Strauss (C.): *Tristes Tropiques*, Plon, 1955.
Anthropologie Structurale, Plon, 1958.

Lin Yu-tang: *My Country My People*.
The Wisdom of China, Michael Joseph, 1944.

Lipmann (Walter): *The Public Philosophy*, Hamish Hamilton, 1955.

Lubac (Henri de): *La Rencontre du Bouddhisme et de l'Occident*, Aubier, 1952.

Mao Tse-tung: *Complete Works. Quotations from Chairman Mao Tse-tung*, Foreign Language Press, Peking, 1966.

Marcel (Gabriel): *La Dignité Humaine*, Aubier Montaigne, 1964.

Margoulies (G.): *La Langue et L'ecriture chinoises*, Payot, 1943.

Maritain (Jacques): *Le Paysan de la Garonne*, Desclée de Brouwer, 1966.

Mauss (Marcel): *Sociologie et Anthropologie*, Presses Universitaires, 1950.

Mende (Tibor): *La Chine et son Ombre*, le Seuil, 1960.
Entre la Peur et l'Espoir, du Seuil, 1958.

Montesquieu: *Les Considérations, L'Esprit des Lois*.

Mounier (Emmanuel): *Introduction aux Existentialismes*, Gallimard, 1962.
Le Personnalisme, Presses Universitaires, 1962.

Mu Fu-sheng: *The Wilting of a Hundred Flowers*, Heinemann, 1962.

Mus (Paul): *Vietnam, Sociologie d'une Guerre*, le Seuil, 1952.

Noel-Baker (The Rt. Hon. Philip): *The Arms Race*, Stevens & Sons, 1958.

Pascal: *Œuvres Complètes*, 1960.

Pinot (Virgile): *La Chine et la Formation de l'Esprit Philosophique en Europe*, Geuthner, 1932.

Purcell (Victor): *The Rise of Modern China*, Routledge, 1962.

Raja Rao: *The Serpent and the Rope*, Murray, 1960.

Rostow (W.W.): *The Stages of Economic Growth*, Cambridge University Press, 1960.

Rygaloff (Alexis): *Confucius*, Presses Universitaires, 1946.

Schram (S.): *Mao Tse-tung*, Armand Colin, 1963.

Schumpeter (Joseph): *Capitalisme, Socialisme et Démocratie*, Payot, 1954.

Siren (Oswald): *The Chinese on the Art of Painting*, Vetch, 1936.

Snow (Edgar): *Red Star Over China*, Random House, 1938.

The Other Side of the River, Random House.

Stein (Rolf): *La Civilisation Tibétaine*, Dunod, 1962.

Teilhard de Chardin: *Le Phénomène Humain*.

Thomas (W.L.): *Current Anthropology*, Chicago University, 1956.

Toynbee (Arnold): *Civilisation on Trial*, Oxford University Press, 1948.

A Study of History, Oxford University Press, 1946.

Waley (Arthur): *Three Ways of Thought in Ancient China*, Allen & Unwin, 1939.

The Way and its Power, Allen & Unwin, 1934.

Zagoria (Donald S.): *The Sino-Soviet Conflict*, Princeton University Press, 1962.

Index

DATE DUE			
REC'D APR 2 8 2006			